These Last Days

These Last Days

A Christian View of History

EDITED BY

RICHARD D. PHILLIPS

and GABRIEL N. E. FLUHRER

P&R PUBLISHING
P.O. BOX 817 • PHILLIPSBURG • NEW JERSEY 08865-0817

Printed in the United States of America

Library of Congress Cataloging-in-Publication Data

Philadelphia Conference on Reformed Theology (36th : 2010)
  These last days : a Christian view of history / edited by Richard D. Phillips and Gabriel N.E. Fluhrer.
      p. cm.
  Papers from the thirty-sixth meeting of the Philadelphia Conference on Reformed Theology held in the spring of 2010.
  Includes bibliographical references.
  ISBN 978-1-59638-251-0 (pbk.)
  1. Eschatology--Congresses. 2. Reformed Church--Doctrines--Congresses. I. Phillips, Richard D. (Richard Davis), 1960- II. Fluhrer, Gabriel N. E., 1978- III. Title.
  BT821.3.P52 2010
  236--dc22
                                        2010053328

To Kenneth R. Wynne,

brother in Christ
and exemplary steward in these last days,
with gratitude

Contents

Editors' Preface

*"Ours is a religion whose centre of gravity
lies beyond the grave in the world to come."*[1]
—Geerhardus Vos

FOR MANY CHRISTIANS, the expression "the last days" refers to the short period of intense activity prior to the second coming of Jesus Christ. But according to the apostles, the last days were inaugurated by the first coming of Christ and continue even today. The book of Hebrews thus begins by saying that while God formerly spoke by the prophets, "in these last days he has spoken to us by his Son" (Heb. 1:2). Paul warned Timothy that "in the last days there will come times of difficulty," and then made it plain that Timothy was living in that very era (2 Tim. 3:1). According to Peter, the last days began with the outpouring of the Spirit at Pentecost. This fulfilled the ancient prophecy that said, "In the last days it shall be, God declares, that I will pour out my Spirit on all flesh" (Acts 2:17). Biblically, for us, the last

1. Geerhardus Vos, *Grace and Glory* (1922; repr., Edinburgh: Banner of Truth Trust, 1994), 165.

days are *these last days*, as we are those, Paul said, "on whom the end of the ages has come" (1 Cor. 10:11).

How do we biblically understand our time as the final age of world history? What does this mean for our faith? These are a few of the questions that were taken up by the thirty-sixth meeting of the Philadelphia Conference on Reformed Theology during the spring months of 2010, the addresses of which are published in this book. Reformed Christians have often shunned the field of eschatology, surrendering end-times doctrine to more popular (but less biblical) schemes held by other believers. But eschatology is important! It was their Christian doctrine of history that thrilled the first Christian disciples: they realized that with the coming of the "last days" they had entered into the time of the eschatological kingdom that dawned with the coming of Christ. Our faith will likewise be strengthened by a biblical view of eschatology and a right understanding of what it means to live in "the present evil age" (Gal. 1:4) by means of "the powers of the age to come" (Heb. 6:5).

This book, like the conference that produced its chapters, attempts to work through biblical eschatology in a more or less chronological fashion. The volume begins with an introductory chapter, "The Christ of History," by Sinclair Ferguson, which articulates why for Reformed Christians the purpose of history is disclosed in the person and work of Christ. After that beginning, the next two chapters ground the reader in the two dimensions of our present age of history. First, believers live in "This Present Evil Age," which D. A. Carson explains with an excellent treatment of the book of Revelation, centered on the symbolic history of Revelation 12. (This chapter alone is worth the price of this book, lucidly displaying the riches of the Apocalypse for those with the hermeneutical eyes to see!) Next, Alistair Begg describes our present era as it is experienced by the church in light of Christ's gift at Pentecost, in "The Age of the Spirit." These two chapters help believers to see the two poles of our current era of history, defined as it is by the struggle between the kingdom of Christ and the kingdom of Satan and the world. Looking forward in time, we are shown the hope that we have in Christ in Michael S. Horton's chapter, "The Resurrection Hope," and J. Ligon Duncan's exposition of "The Eternal Glory" that awaits believers in Christ. Finally, D. A. Carson applies the whole of Reformed eschatology to the believer's present experience in "Partakers of the Age of Come."

Included in this book are some of the outstanding seminars that enriched our conference. All readers will be informed by these chapters, but some of them are likely to be particularly appreciated by different readers. Cornelis P. Venema's lucid comparison of "The Four Main Millennial Views," Richard D. Phillips's presentation of "A Pastoral Guide to Life after Death," and Jeffrey K. Jue's tour of "Evangelical Eschatology, American Style," are likely to be particularly valued. Finally, Paul David Tripp gives us his trademark applied theology in "The Radical Implications of Eternity."

As we were preparing this conference on Reformed eschatology, we were frequently asked which millennial view was being promoted: premillennial, amillennial, or postmillennial? At the time, we answered honestly that there was no attempt to promote a single view or isolate the others, and that we did not even know the millennial position of all the participants. Time has shown, however, that the material in this book consistently espouses the amillennial view of eschatology. The fact that this predominance was unintentional shows all the more clearly the growing espousal of this view in Reformed circles. To this effect, the editors wish gratefully to acknowledge the impressive contributions of Cornel Venema, Kim Riddlebarger,

Samuel Waldron, and especially the late Geerhardus Vos, apart from whose labors Reformed Christians might still be anguishing in fear of "these last days."

Lastly, the editors wish gratefully to acknowledge Robert Brady and the outstanding staff of the Alliance of Confessing Evangelicals, whose tireless labors enable us to continue the historic legacy of the Philadelphia Conference on Reformed Theology; the congregation and session of Second Presbyterian Church in Greenville, South Carolina, where the editors have labored in a shared gospel ministry; and the editors and staff of P&R Publishing, with whom we consider it a privilege to work and publish. Most importantly, we offer these chapters to the Lord of history, the Savior who reigns over both heaven and earth during these last days, and for whose glorious return we join with the apostle John in eager prayer, saying, "Come, Lord Jesus!" Amen.

Gabriel N. E. Fluhrer
Richard D. Phillips
November 2010

1

The Christ of History

SINCLAIR FERGUSON

I will put enmity between you and the woman,
and between your offspring and her offspring.
(Genesis 3:15)

THE CHRIST OF HISTORY—what a grand theme!
While there are many, many places we could go in Scripture
to expound such a theme, I would like to focus on the well-
known fifteenth verse of the third chapter of Genesis. However,
before we look at that verse, it may be helpful to be reminded
of the context.

Adam and Eve have sinned and eaten of the fruit of the tree
of the knowledge of good and evil, from which God had forbid-
den them to eat. He has exposed them and is pronouncing a
series of judgments on them. In verses 14–19, he begins with
the serpent, then moves on to Eve, and then to Adam.

Starting with Genesis 3:15

God's word to the serpent in Genesis 3:15 is this: "I will put enmity between you and the woman, and between your offspring and her offspring; he shall bruise your head, and you shall bruise his heel." How does this relate to the Christ of history? To answer that question, we need to turn forward to the New Testament.

For many of us, a favorite passage in the Gospels is Luke 24. There Luke gives us an account of the conversation that our Lord had with the weary and sad disciples on the road to Emmaus. Luke tells us that the disciples experienced three things. First, they experienced the Lord Jesus opening the Scriptures to them. Second, they experienced the Holy Spirit opening their minds, so that they could understand them. Third, and finally, they experienced their hearts burning within them as the stranger expounded the Scriptures to them. They exclaimed, "Did not our hearts burn within us while he talked to us on the road, while he opened to us the Scriptures?" (v. 32). Surely we would love to have been passers-by who could walk five, ten, or fifteen paces behind those three as they went to Emmaus, to listen to the Lord Jesus teaching the whole Bible!

Why do I bring this story up? Because, over the years, I have become more and more convinced that Jesus began with this verse in Genesis 3. The church has historically proclaimed that Genesis 3:15 contains the *Protoevangelium*—the "first gospel," or the first gospel promise. It is a particularly striking promise because it is actually a word of judgment spoken to the serpent, and not in the first instance spoken either to Adam or Eve. And it is also striking because it speaks more of victory than it does of pardon and forgiveness. Now, to be sure, the rest of the Scripture will underscore for us that pardon and forgiveness are anything but incidental; indeed, pardon and forgiveness are absolutely essential to the conquest that is ultimately ascribed here to the Lord Jesus Christ. But the word in Genesis 3:15 is a word of judgment, enmity, alienation, and opposition. "I will put enmity between you (the serpent) and the woman, and between your seed and her seed; he shall bruise your head, and you shall bruise his heel," God says.

Let us turn to the New Testament again to see how it views what is so closely related to this event, namely, the person and work of our Lord Jesus Christ. If you are sensitive to the language of Scripture and I were to ask you, "What is the reason the Son of God came into the world?" you would immediately quote the words of 1 John 3:8: "The reason the Son of God appeared was to destroy the works of the devil." You might also think of the words of the apostle Paul in Colossians 2:14–15, where he speaks about Christ taking the bond of guilt that stood against us and nailing it to the cross, turning the cross, as Calvin said, into "a signal trophy or show of triumph, in which Christ led about his enemies."[1] Or you might call to mind Hebrews 2:14–15, which speaks about Christ taking our human nature, sharing our flesh in order that he might destroy the one who has the power of death, the devil, and release all those who through fear of death were in lifelong bondage and subjection to the devil.

Thus, there is a sense in which the sentiment of A. N. Whitehead, that the whole of Western philosophy is simply a series of footnotes to Plato, could be applied to the Bible. We could say that it is simply a series of extended expressions, footnotes, and expositions of this word of conflict in Genesis 3:15—and ultimately of Christ's final victory over the serpent. This theme is dramatically picked up at the end of the book of Revelation,

1. John Calvin, *Commentary on Philippians, Colossians, and Thessalonians*.

where the serpent has grown large through much devouring of the sons and daughters of Adam and Eve. He has been transformed, as it were, into a giant serpent, a red dragon who sweeps from the sky a third of its stars. He becomes not only the prince of the power of the air, but the god of this age. Here the promise given in Genesis 3:15 is painted in vivid colors to describe the way in which its consummation is found in Jesus Christ, who is the Christ of history and the Lord of time and eternity.

So, in this chapter, I want us to gather some of those biblical footnotes together. This will feel almost as though we were racing through the pages of a study Bible and pausing at texts here and there to see how marvelously, from beginning to end, our Lord Jesus Christ is set before us. I want to do this so that we may see him in his glory. Although we do not yet see everything under his feet, when we read the Bible we are to see Jesus, to learn that God has placed all things under his feet and that one day his triumph and final victory will be visible from the ends of the earth.

Christ the Meaning of History

Here is the first principle I want us to think about: Genesis 3:15 shows us that Jesus Christ himself is the meaning of history. Perhaps you have heard (what some consider to be) a trite phrase like, "History is HIS story." I remember hearing that as a young Christian and feeling somewhat creepy about the whole idea that somebody would take a word like *history* and try to turn it into a piece of theology by a form of allegory. And yet I suppose the power of the illustration is evident in the fact that I still remember it so many years later! It is true, you know. Our history really is Jesus Christ's story. It is not about us—although, in God's providence and saving grace, he is *for* us. But it is a story written about him, and the story is set up in Genesis 3:15 as the story of world conflict. It is about the conflict between the seed of the serpent and the seed of the woman, which will find its ultimate consummation in a personal conflict. In this battle, the serpent will crush the heel of the seed (plural) of the woman, and the seed (singular) of the woman will himself crush the head of the serpent.

The whole of history is, from the beginning of the book of Genesis to the end of the book of Revelation, a story told through the lens of the struggle between these two antithetical powers. Whether it is Cain versus Abel, or God versus the Tower of Babel, or the Israelites versus the Egyptians, or Goliath versus David, or Babylon versus Jerusalem, or Jesus versus the Pharisees, or the early Christians versus the Roman Empire—in one form or another, the Bible invites us to understand that the basic theme of all human history is, as Augustine famously said, the story of the City of God being built in the context of the City of Man trying to do its best to destroy it.

Here in Genesis, a collective antagonism is revealed, one seed in opposition to another seed. But it is a story that leads to a grand day, a final climax, when the two great protagonists will face off: Satan, who speaks through the serpent, versus our Lord Jesus Christ. But this happens presently until this great climax. Both the Old Testament and the New Testament make it absolutely clear that, in this world, we can expect a story of kingdom against kingdom, Jesus against the serpent, the City of God against the City of the World. But injected into that conflict right from the very beginning is this amazing promise of a personal Redeemer, a Savior who is to come. He will come and conquer the one who is the father of all our woes. He will bring such a great deliverance from the power of sin that, from the very earliest moments following the fall in the garden of Eden, the hope that was injected into the hearts of our first parents still burns brightly and never disappears. No matter how often it is attacked in human history, the hope of the coming Redeemer, whom we know now to be our Lord Jesus Christ, still burns as bright as ever.

I rather think that this is at least part of what Eve says in Genesis 4:1: "I have gotten a man with the help of the LORD." Was this the promised Redeemer, coming so quickly? Sadly, it was not. But the hope continued. In Genesis 5:28–29, we read that Lamech called his son's name Noah, saying, "Out of the ground that the LORD has cursed this one shall bring us relief from our work and from the painful toil of our hands." Fascinatingly, the theme of rest will continue to loom large over the entire Old Testament. God persists in promising to his people that one day he will bring the rest that was typified in Noah. But it is never actualized in the Old Testament, so that even when the prophet Isaiah looks back on the exodus as a great picture of God's saving deliverance from the city of this world and victory for the kingdom of God, he speaks about the way in which the people resisted the fact that the Holy Spirit of God had come in that event to give them a measure of rest from the curse.

From Noah, the story continues in the promise given to Abraham. There is that strange scene in Genesis 22, where Abraham's son Isaac says, "Behold, the fire and the wood, but where is the lamb for a burnt offering?" (v. 7). Then Abraham, in a wonderfully prophetic way, assures his own seed—who was himself given supernaturally as a kind of prototype of the supernatural giving of the blessed Son of God—that "God will provide for himself the lamb for a burnt offering, my son" (v. 8). Thus Abraham's hand was stayed because of the ram, caught in a thicket (v. 13).

So the pictures begin to build up in the Old Testament Scriptures. God gives his people priests and promises that one day there will be a priest after the order of Melchizedek, whose priesthood will consummate all priesthood. As God's believing people stand and watch the priests making the daily sacrifices, they are supposed to think, "This cannot possibly be the sacrifice that God has promised to take away sins! Else, why are the sacrifices repeated day after day?" So, year after year, the longings of God's people are drawn out and a deep-seated desire begins to grow that all of this will come to its promised consummation.

They are given kings, and their prophets speak about how the coming King will reign from one end of the world to the other. His reign will bring *shalom*, or peace, a sense of wholeness and completion. They begin to speak about how this coming King will crush all his enemies under his feet, how his reign will be a reign of plentiful joy and pardon and restoration and power and reconciliation and worship.

But it was not just a great King that was promised—a Prophet, greater than Moses, was also promised (Deut. 18:18). The people, since Moses, surely wondered, "Who will speak God's word in power and in truth, as coming from the very presence of God and seeing the face of God and tasting the glory of God?" This burning question also remained to be answered.

Then there were the strange figures that the prophet Isaiah and the prophet Daniel saw in their visions. As Isaiah looks toward the coming day when the people of God will be in bondage in hated Babylon, he sees that geographical restoration is not their deepest need. No, their deepest need is still for the promise of Genesis 3:15 to be fulfilled. So Isaiah speaks of one who would be so exalted that kings would shut their mouths because of him. At the end of Isaiah 52 and into chapter 53—the beginning of the Fourth Servant Song—Isaiah speaks of the one who would sprinkle many nations, yet would himself be wounded and crushed. He would be crushed for the sins of his people and then exalted and share his spoil with the strong.

Daniel sees the Son of Man, the son of Adam who would come to the Ancient of Days and share his kingdom with the saints of the Most High (Dan. 7:13–14). All history is laid in tribute to this single purpose of God—all that takes place among the nations that rise and fall serves his glorious purpose—so that one day he who has spoken in many and fragmentary ways to our fathers through the prophets would in the last days speak through his Son. The whole story of the Bible, then, is the story of Jesus Christ. He is the meaning of history.

Of course, the implication of all this is that, though we may find out many things in this world, if we leave out Jesus Christ, we will ultimately be left in a state of frustration because we lack this world's unifying principle. Isn't this what the scientists and historians discover as they struggle with the basic material of their respective disciplines? The greatest of them have always longed to find something that would unify the whole. The famous physicist Stephen Hawking has been seeking this unifying principle for most of his life. The amazing thing is that the simplest reader of the Scriptures knows the answer! Jesus Christ is the meaning of the cosmos, and Jesus Christ is the meaning of history.

Christ the Center of History

In the second place, Jesus Christ is not only the meaning of history, but also the center of history. Therefore, the story of Herod's pogrom (Matt. 2:16) is not something to be read in isolation from the promise of Genesis 3:15. Herod is the agent of the serpent who seeks to bruise the heel of the seed of the woman.

This theme is woven deeply into the story of Jesus' life, as it is recorded in both the Synoptic Gospels and John: the goal of his life and ministry is to plant a church in enemy-occupied territory. Therefore, the full force of the enemy is focused upon Jesus himself.

Think of the temptation narratives in Matthew 4:1–11 or Luke 4:1–13. We often read these sections of Scripture with the question in mind of how to relate Jesus' temptations to our own struggles with temptation. We then ask how we can learn to overcome temptation by the way Jesus overcame temptation.

While this is certainly not wrong at all, it is not the point of the narrative to answer these kinds of questions. This is because, interestingly, temptations don't come to Jesus. Rather, Jesus goes to be tempted. He is led there, driven into the wilderness by the Holy Spirit. Perhaps the really significant thing about Jesus' temptations is not the way in which they are like ours, but the way in which they are fundamentally unique.

Arguably the most significant of these unique temptations is the temptation from the devil simply to worship him. In return for this, Satan will give Jesus the kingdoms of this world. Why should this tempt Jesus? Because he came for the kingdoms of this world! He came to undo the disaster and tragedy that Adam had effected. Adam had been set in the garden; it was almost as though God did for Adam what a kind father would do for his own son. God gave him a little start; the whole world was not yet the paradise that God commanded Adam to make it. The garden was demarcated from the rest of the world, but God gave his son Adam a little start. He said to Adam, "Here is a garden. Your task is to tend this garden and to expand this garden until it fills the whole earth." Strikingly, God commanded Adam to do this until, as it were, all the kingdoms of this world were his.

If Adam had done that, just like a child who accomplishes something even though his father gave him a significant start, he would have brought it all back to his Father and said, "Father, look what I have done! I want you to have it all!" So Adam's fall was not just a matter of personal sin; it was a matter of cosmic disaster. He lost the world and Satan gained it—that's why the Scriptures insist that Satan is the god of this age, the prince of this world who needs to be cast out.

In his temptation of our Lord, Satan, in effect, says to Jesus, "I will give you exactly what you have come for, only on my terms." The breathtaking marvel is that Jesus refuses the very thing for which he has come, in order that, in gaining that for which he has come, he might crush the head of the serpent rather than bow down at the serpent's feet. This is why, when Jesus emerges triumphant from the wilderness, Luke writes this: "And when the devil had ended every temptation, he departed from him until an opportune time" (4:13). In other words, much of the early stages of the gospel narratives are about all hell quite literally being let loose against Jesus.

We mustn't be under the misapprehension that the whole Bible is a book about demons running loose all over the place. The Bible rarely speaks about demons, and demons rarely appear in the thousands of years of Bible history. But they appear in massive force in that little land of Palestine around the year 30 AD. Why? Because the kingdom of darkness is tottering. Think of the Gadarene demonic (Mark 5:1–20). Here is a poor man running around like a maniac, cutting himself with stones, living among the tombs. He is so vicious that no one can bind him, even with chains. When asked for his name, he says it is "Legion, for we are many." It only takes one demon to destroy a man's life, so why are there so many tormenting this man? Because the King has come to reclaim his territory, and the demons are massing to oppose him.

Meanwhile, Jesus is marching forward, having dealt in measure with Satan's first temptations. What is so fascinating in the temptation narrative is that the whole demonic, satanic pressure seems to be employed to keep Jesus away from the cross. Satan is saying, "You can have the kingdoms—just don't go to the cross." He may have reasoned, "Let's expose who Jesus is, and he will never be able to go the cross." Remarkably, it is Simon Peter, of all people, who suggests the latter: "Never to the cross, Lord!" What is Jesus' reply? "Get behind me, Satan!" (Matt. 16:23). I wonder if it is significant that when Peter fails as the instrument of the powers of darkness, Satan changes his tactic. Instead of seeking to divert Jesus from the cross, Satan seeks to put Jesus on the cross in his time and in his way through Judas Iscariot. So much so is this the case that, when Jesus is arrested, he says, "But this is your hour, and the power of darkness" (Luke 22:53).

From every human point of view, it seemed that Satan's victory was consummated when Jesus was crucified. In this respect, the cross seemed to advance the plan of sinful man and Satan, not the plan of God. This would appear to be true—except that Jesus gave little clues as he has fulfilled his ministry. "See, we are going up to Jerusalem. And the Son of Man will be delivered over to the chief priests . . . to be mocked and flogged and crucified" (Matt. 20:18–19). "Now is the judgment of this world; now will the ruler of this world be cast out" (John 12:31). And though the very epicenter of history is contained in the few last days of his earthly ministry, our Lord Jesus Christ's heel was crushed, as he entered into this dark world of conflict with the power of darkness in a fulfillment of Genesis 3:15. Thus, the hymn writer can exclaim, "Well might the sun in darkness hide, and shut his glories in, when Christ, the mighty Maker died for man, the creature's sin!"[2] These words are only fitting as Christ entered into the alienation and agony of Calvary.

How better could Satan have triumphed, given this awful scene at the foot of the cross? There Jesus was, feeling the awful sense of alienation from his heavenly Father and bearing the judgment of God against our sin. His very Father placed sin upon him and then judged him as though he were the sinner! Surely, at the cross, it was Satan more than anyone else who might have cried, "It is finished!"

Satan did not realize that, by tasting death for us and rising again in power and glory, our Lord Jesus Christ would bring about the pardon of our sins according to the righteous judgment of God. Therefore, Jesus removed the power of sin and death that Satan, as it were, held over us. Satan was utterly defeated when he thought he was the most triumphant.

Jesus did not simply die, get placed in a tomb, and rise again from the dead a few moments later. No, he was in the tomb for three days. And this was not just in fulfillment of prophecy—to be sure, it was that, but not only that. It was because he really tasted death (and all that death carries with it) in such a way that his own supporters—if we can call them that—might well have believed that the enemy had won the victory. In fact, however, what was happening was that all the powers of death and hell were being exhausted in Jesus. As he rose again from the grave, he left the symbols of the conflict in the grave itself and rose in majestic glory and in power.

I have always been fascinated by the fact that Mary Magdalene was standing there forlornly in the garden, mourning the death of Jesus. (Now, we should pause here and notice something amazing before we continue. Our story, as human beings, began in

---

2. Isaac Watts, "Alas! And Did My Savior Bleed" (1707).

a garden. Adam turned the garden into a wilderness, and Jesus went into the wilderness to deal with the enemy, in order that he might turn the world back into a garden again. Isn't that wonderful to think about?)

To return to Mary in the garden: John, who seems to love double entendres, records that Mary saw Jesus and supposed him to be the gardener (John 20:15). Jesus wanted her to see him like that, but it wasn't just that little space that he was gardening. By his resurrection, he was "gardening" the whole cosmos. Jesus Christ is the center of history.

Christ the Lord of History

Third, we must also see that Christ is the Lord of history. Simon Peter illustrates this well. Isn't it amazing to read about the transformation in Simon Peter after the resurrection? What happens to him? Well, first he receives roughly a six-week seminar on how to read the Bible. Can you imagine Jesus teaching you how to read the Bible? After this, Peter appears on the day of Pentecost, preaching as though all his life he has been meditating on the way in which the Scriptures, pointing to the Lord Jesus Christ, fit together. Among the many marvelous things he says on the day of Pentecost, this is what I want to focus on: "Let all the house of Israel therefore know for certain that God has made him both Lord and Christ, this Jesus whom you crucified" (Acts 2:36).

According to Peter here, Jesus is Lord. He is the Son of God. Peter doesn't mean that the heavenly Father has exalted the Lord Jesus to deity. Instead, what he seems to mean is that God originally made Adam to be Lord, but Adam failed. Now Jesus has gone into the wilderness, has begun to turn that into a garden, has defeated the powers of darkness, and has been raised up to the throne of heaven and declared by the heavenly Father to be Lord of this earth. His work is finished, and restoration is absolutely guaranteed.

Because Jesus is Lord, several things follow. First of all, his word of gospel grace is to be proclaimed to the ends of the earth. "Go therefore and make disciples of all nations." Why? Because "all authority in heaven and on earth has been given to me," Jesus says (Matt. 28:18–19). This is the way in which the Father has fulfilled his promise to his Son: "Ask of me, and I will make the nations your heritage, and the ends of the earth your possession" (Ps. 2:8). In the Great Commission, then, Jesus says to his disciples, in effect, "Go and claim my inheritance, continue to garden, spread the seed of the gospel, bring them in, and I who am the Lord of history will be with you till the end of the age."

In the second place, notice that our Lord Jesus, who has crushed the head of the serpent, has not imagined that the crushing of his head will be the end of the battle. While he is the Lord of history and thus guarantees our victory, it is not the end of the battle. So he says to his disciples, "I will build my church, and the gates of hell shall not prevail against it" (Matt. 16:18). But there is still struggle, so that we see the blood of martyrs and even the struggle in our own congregations against the dark powers. This is because, as Paul puts it, "We do not wrestle against flesh and blood, but against the rulers, against the authorities, against the cosmic powers over this present darkness, against the spiritual forces of evil in the heavenly places" (Eph. 6:12).

It is interesting to note how Paul opens Ephesians and closes Ephesians by telling us that we have been raised up in Christ into the heavenly places. And it is precisely in this new order of reality that the battle is fiercest, because we don't wrestle against flesh and blood. So the Lord of history, our Lord Jesus Christ, sends us to the nations, wearing gospel armor that he himself has tried and proved because he knows that the ongoing battle will be bloody. But he means to extend the gospel to the ends of the earth and to the end of the age.

It is Paul, after all, who gives us a most wonderful glimpse into how Jesus Christ will finally show himself to be the Lord of history in that great chapter of his on the resurrection, 1 Corinthians 15. From verse 20 onward, he gives us, as it were, a little synopsis of the whole story. He tells us that "Christ has been raised from the dead, the firstfruits of those who have fallen asleep" (1 Cor. 15:20). And then, at his coming, those who belong to Christ will be raised with him because he must reign until he has made all his enemies a stool for his feet (v. 25).

And then Paul says something stunning in 1 Corinthians 15:27–28:

> For "God has put all things in subjection under his feet." But when it says, "all things are put in subjection," it is plain that he is excepted who put all things in subjection under him. When all things are subjected to him, then the Son himself will also be subjected to him who put all things in subjection under him, that God may be all in all.

What does Paul mean? Does he mean that the eternal Son will, at the end of the day, be subordinated, as a kind of second-order deity, to the heavenly Father, so that God the Father may be the supreme God and the Son a secondary God?

Not at all. Remember the whole context in which Paul is here speaking. The context is the story of the first man and the second man, the first Adam and the last Adam. It's the story we have been following from Genesis 3:15, about how the first man was created with the garden to be expanded into the whole world. When he had become Lord of the whole world, he would bring it back to the heavenly Father, presumably with his many descendants, and say: "Here am I, Father, and all the children you have given me, and we have finished the work that you gave us to do. We present this as our thankful love offering to you with the adoration of all our hearts."

What Paul is saying is that what Adam failed to do, our Lord Jesus Christ has begun to do and will finally accomplish. When every knee is bowed to him, when the lion lies down with the lamb, when the blind see, and the dead are raised, and the dumb speak, and the deaf hear, and the cripples run and dance, and all of the elect of God are gathered together, resurrected, restored, sanctified, and made like Jesus Christ, then the victory will be complete. As the second Adam, he will lead us all to the throne of his heavenly Father and say, "Here we are, Father." You and I will be hiding behind him, proclaiming that we did nothing to contribute to this. He will be saying, "Here am I and the children you have given me, and in their name I present this glorified world to you as our love offering. Since you have in your good pleasure deemed that I should take their nature and their name, I, on their behalf, bring the whole of history and all its glorious purposes for the salvation of these, my dear ones, to you. Together we bow before you." That's at least something that Paul was getting at.

We do not yet see Jesus as Lord of all because we do not yet see all things under his feet. So where are we to look? You have to look at Jesus. Because, you see, he is not only the Lord of all history, but the Lord of my history.

My congregation in Columbia, South Carolina, must think that I do not know how to end sermons. This is because I always end the same way. Let me end that way here: don't you think it is the greatest thing in the world to be a Christian?

2

This Present Evil Age

D. A. CARSON

She gave birth to a male child, one who is to rule
all the nations with a rod of iron, but her child was
caught up to God and to his throne.
(Revelation 12:5)

WHEN MY SON was about three years old, I asked him one day where he had gotten his deep, blue eyes. He responded (with all the authority that he could muster) that he had received them from God. Of course, he was right. If he had been twenty-one and a biology student, he might have answered that he had them because, although neither I nor his mother had blue eyes, both of us must have passed on to him the necessary recessive gene for blue eyes!

I tell this story only to provoke a question: which answer is more true? We can ask the same question when we look in the

17

Bible at what caused the destruction of the southern kingdom of Judah in 587 BC. One could mention the rise of the regional superpower Babylon, combined with the decline and decay of the Davidic dynasty. Or we might talk about the criminal stupidity of Zedekiah, despite Jeremiah's warnings. Or we might look at the sins of the people, sins that attracted God's judgment. Or we could simply say that God caused it. Which of these answers is the most true? Well, they are equally true.

Thinking in terms of contemporary Christianity, we could ask what causes the church around the world her greatest difficulties, sufferings, and troubles. The answers would be different in different parts of the world. For example, the church in Africa struggles against militant Islam and the AIDS epidemic. One could similarly move to Latin America, Europe, or North America and see different struggles. There is the rising secularization of all these places—philosophical pluralism, moral indifferentism, and hedonism. In the church, we see doctrinal indifference, carelessness, and a lack of love.

But I have noticed that all the categories for problems today are sociological, psychological, or related to demographics. Do not misunderstand me, for I am certainly not saying that there is nothing to be learned from sociological analysis. There is a huge amount to be learned from the discipline. But trouble arises when all of our descriptions of what is right or wrong in the world follow only those paradigms. This causes us to look for solutions from places like sociology, and that is a huge mistake. Moreover, this analysis doesn't penetrate behind the sociological and cultural phenomena to the God who still remains in charge. It disregards the God whose word we have to help us understand the phenomena that are taking place around us.

The Rage of Satan

In the book of Revelation, chapter 12, God gives us a deeper analysis of the difficulties and sufferings of the church on this side of the coming of Christ. Before the final display of wrath in the seven plagues of chapter 16, chapters 12–14 mark a major division in the book. Here we find the underlying cause for the hostility and suffering that will fall upon the world. They also explain the conflict between the world and the church. Thus, if we are going to understand this present evil age, this is a very good place to begin.

First, John outlines the occasion for the satanic malice that characterizes this chapter. He traces all the problems that Christians now face to Satan's rage. The devil is filled with fury because he knows his time is short. John outlines this rage in verses 1–9. The scene opens with a sign. As he does in other places, John here uses the language of a sign to point in some way to the consummation, the content of the spectacle itself. But let us look at what Revelation 12:1–2 says:

> And a great sign appeared in heaven: a woman clothed with the sun, with the moon under her feet, and on her head a crown of twelve stars. She was pregnant and was crying out in birth pains and the agony of giving birth.

The question naturally arises: who is this woman? Many have argued across the centuries that she is married, because she gives birth to a male child who will rule all the nations with an iron scepter (vv. 5–6). Now, that transparently refers to Jesus, but this woman is not married. Rather, John is here referring to the messianic community, whether under the old covenant or under the new. Just as Zion or Jerusalem is the mother of the people of God in the Old Testament, so in the New Testament the Jerusalem above is our mother (Gal. 4:26). The Messiah comes out of this messianic community.

This community began with the calling of Abraham and the constituting of the nation. Now it continues in a new form, under the terms of the new covenant. This becomes obvious when you get down to the end of the chapter, for the offspring of the woman are those who keep God's commands and hold fast their testimony about Jesus. These cannot be married! So this is a reference to the church, the church of the living God, which is the ongoing messianic community.

John further tells us that she is utterly radiant. The imagery of her feet on the moon suggests dominion of some sort. We are also told that she has on her head a crown of twelve stars. The number twelve is vitally important to the book of Revelation. Jesus himself links the twelve apostles with the twelve tribes, which constitute the entirety of God's holy covenant people from the old and new covenants.

The description continues in verse 2, as she is described as being pregnant and in great travail. She is undergoing what Jews came to refer to as "the birth pains of the Messiah." This notion was rooted in the Old Testament. For example, in Isaiah 26:17 we read, "Like a pregnant woman who writhes and cries out in her pangs when she is near to giving birth, so were we because of you, O LORD." So what we have here is the true Israel in an agony of suffering and expectation as the Messiah is born.

The second sign in the spectacle is an enormous red dragon. Look at verses 3 and 4:

> And another sign appeared in heaven: behold, a great red
> dragon, with seven heads and ten horns, and on his heads seven

diadems. His tail swept down a third of the stars of heaven and cast them to the earth. And the dragon stood before the woman who was about to give birth, so that when she bore her child he might devour it.

Now, in case we are in any doubt as to the identity of the serpent, John removes it in verse 9: "And the great dragon was thrown down, that ancient serpent, who is called the devil and Satan." The apostle here picks up the language of Genesis 3 and tells us that the dragon is in the guise of the serpent. Satan is also identified with Leviathan or Behemoth in the Old Testament. Satan has many guises, and he uses them all. These forms or representations are all symbolic of, and connected with, all that opposes God.

Think of Peter in Matthew 16:14–23. Right after he gives the apostolic confession concerning Christ's identity, Jesus announces that he must go to Jerusalem and die. Peter, thinking that since he has scored once theologically he should try again, says, "Never!" But Jesus wheels on him and says, "Get behind me, Satan!" This passage is not saying that Peter is demon-possessed. What the Bible is telling us is that this was not really Peter speaking. His judgment is so mistaken that he actually serves as Satan's mouthpiece. So Satan himself can stand behind nations, regional empires, world orders, and even an apostle.

Here in Revelation 12, he is a red dragon, probably indicating murderousness. He has seven heads like Leviathan in Psalm 74:14, which is a way of signaling the universality of his power. The ten horns recall the fourth beast of Daniel 7. He has crowns on his head, crowns of authority usurped from him who is described in this book as the Lord of lords and King of kings, the one who has the right to rule with a rod of iron.

The drama itself begins in verses 4–6:

His tail swept down a third of the stars of heaven and cast them to the earth. And the dragon stood before the woman who was about to give birth, so that when she bore her child he might devour it. She gave birth to a male child, one who is to rule all the nations with a rod of iron, but her child was caught up to God and to his throne, and the woman fled into the wilderness, where she has a place prepared by God, in which she is to be nourished for 1,260 days.

The scene is meant to be grotesque. The woman, symbolizing the messianic community, has her feet up in the straps, so to speak, pushing to bring to birth the Messiah that she has carried. There is this hideous monster standing between her legs, waiting to grab the baby as it emerges from the womb and eat it. That is the picture here.

The Woman and Her Worthy Son

But then there are two further symbolic elements that need to be unpacked. We are told in verse 6 that the woman flees into the wilderness for 1,260 days. She has given birth to a male child who will rule all the nations with an iron scepter, and her child has been snatched up to God and his throne. So, in one verse, we move from his birth to his childhood to the onset of his public ministry to the years of public ministry. This finally issues in his death, burial, resurrection, and ascension to the right hand of the Majesty on high. There he already reigns at God's right hand. We begin to say to ourselves, "Why is the author skipping over all the important parts?"

But he has covered them! You must read chapters 1–11 to see this. Already in chapters 4 and 5, the significance of the Son has been set forth. Chapter 4 is to chapter 5 what a setting is to a drama. In chapter 4, we are given a picture of the transcendence of God in highly symbolic terms. His "otherness" is set forth as the one who is the sole Creator. He is the one before whom even the highest angels bow down and cover their faces, not daring to gaze on the holiness of his majesty. They cry, "Holy, holy, holy, Lord God Almighty," picking up the language of the great vision in Isaiah 6.

Once this is established, the drama begins in Revelation 5. In the right hand of him who sits on the throne is a scroll, and this scroll is sealed with seven seals. As the book of Revelation unfolds, it becomes transparent that this book contains all of God's purposes for judgment and blessing. And, in the symbolism of the day, to take a scroll and break its seals was to bring to pass whatever was written on the scroll. That's how these things come to pass in what we call history.

Then a loud-voiced angel cries to the entire universe, "Who is worthy to open the scroll and break its seals?" (Rev. 5:2). And now the significance of the setting is clear: this is not a God before whom you just saunter on in, saying, "Oh, God, let me just volunteer for you." Here is the God before whom even the highest angels cover their faces and dare not to look at the blazing glory. Who is going to saunter into his presence and volunteer?

The answer, we are told, is that no one was found who was worthy—not an angel, not an earthbound dweller, not a necromancer, not one from the abodes of the dead. So John weeps, and he weeps because he wants to take a peek into the future. But God says no. He weeps because, in the symbolism of the vision, he sees that unless the seals of that book are opened, all of God's purposes for judgment and blessing will not come to pass. Thus, the church would be suffering for nothing. There is no guarantee of any just end to all of this. There is no guarantee that the balances will be set aright on the last day. There is no assurance that justice will be done and will be seen to be done. The whole thing is meaningless. History is meaningless. Suffering is meaningless.

But the interpreting elder taps John on the shoulder and says to him, "Stop your crying. Look, the Lion of the tribe of Judah has prevailed to open the scroll" (see Rev. 5:5). So John looks and sees a Lamb. Now, you must understand that apocalyptic literature loves to mingle its metaphors. You are not to think of two animals parked side by side, a lion and lamb. The Lion *is* the Lamb—that's the point. The Lion of the tribe of Judah, the messianic figure from David's line, is also a sacrificial Lamb. Yet, at the same time, he is a Lamb with a perfection of seven horns, which symbolizes all kingly authority. Furthermore, this Lamb doesn't come from the outside and have to approach this terrifying God. He himself comes to the throne. He is one with God and, as a result of his sacrifice, he calls together men and woman from every tongue and tribe and people and nation. He gathers around the throne those singing to him who sits on the throne and to himself, the Lamb. This is not merely a song of creation, but a new song, a song of redemption.

Now, remember that all of this is taking place before chapter 12, so that when we reach 12:5, all of this must be in the back of our minds. We are now focusing on the church, this woman who has brought to birth the Messiah and who is still left here with her children. But the Messiah himself is now at God's own right hand. So John wants us to focus on what happens to the woman next.

We are told that she flees to the desert for 1,260 days. What does that mean? Consider the desert, first of all. In Old Testament symbolism, the desert, the wilderness, has two foci, which complete and sometimes complement each other. The desert is the place of wilderness before entry into the Promised Land. So there is a sense in which we, as the church, are now in a kind of desert before the consummation takes place. We are still not in the consummation; that happens in the new heavens and earth.

Also, in the prophecy of Hosea, the desert is given wonderful and rich symbolism. Hosea is the prophet who pictures God as a betrayed husband. He is betrayed by his own people, and yet this God is so tender, so loving, so inherently faithful to his own covenant promises, that he thinks of his people. He says, "Therefore, behold, I will allure her, and bring her into the wilderness, and speak tenderly to her" (Hos. 2:14). He does this because the wilderness was also the place where God, in preparing his people for the land of promise, cared for and protected them, providing them food—quail, even, and all the manna necessary. There God disclosed himself in glory over the tabernacle, leading them and protecting them. So the wilderness is the place where there is opposition and terror. It is also the place where God carefully nurtures and prepares his people before the dawning of the messianic age.

Trial and Triumph in the Wilderness

What about the 1,260 days? In fact, there are four expressions that occur in chapters 12, 13, and 14. The 1,260 days are the equivalent of forty-two idealized months of thirty days each. Forty-two months is the same as three and a half years, which is

25

the same as one time (year), two more, and half a time. These, then, are all the same way of expressing the same thing: (1) time, times, and half a time, (2) three and a half years, (3) forty-two months, and (4) 1,260 days.

What does this mean? The primary controlling figure, I suspect, is the crucial three and a half years of pagan tyranny led by Antiochus Epiphanes. In the history of many countries, some period of time or some date is so bound up with their self-identity that any citizen of that country hearing of that date or that period of time calls to mind all of the associations. Thus, if you hear the phrase "Four score and seven years ago," is there any American reader who doesn't know what I am referring to? If you have been brought up in the American school system, you know that I am referring to Lincoln's Gettysburg Address, that famous speech that captured so much and so little. Or, if you are British, if I speak of the year 1066, you know what I am referring to. That was the year when the Normans won at the Battle of Hastings, when the entire direction of the British Isles changed.

So, here, three and a half years was by this time figuring hugely in Jewish self-consciousness. After Alexander the Great died, his mighty Greek empire extended from Greece all the way to the borders of India. It was then divided up amongst four generals. One was called Ptolemy, and he took over Egypt. A little farther north was the Seleucid Dynasty that took over what is now Syria. So little Israel was squashed between the Seleucids to the north and the Ptolemies to the south. It thus became the plaything of both, really a no-man's-land.

Eventually the Seleucids took over, and there arose in their dynasty Antiochus IV, also known as Antiochus Epiphanes. He decided that little Israel had to be paganized. So, in 167 BC, he marched in with his troops and slaughtered pigs in the temple. He then made it a capital offense to observe the Sabbath. He further made it a capital offense to own any copy of the Torah. He determined to slaughter all the priests.

But in the hill country there was an old man with three sons. He killed the first of the emissaries sent by the Seleucids. After this, his older son Judas started conducting guerrilla warfare. We have pages and pages of information about these events from the first-century writer Josephus. Judas came to be called "the Hammer." His name, then, was Judas the Hammer or Judas Maccabeus, and hence we come to what is known as the Maccabean revolt.

For three and a half bloody years, they kept fighting the Seleucids until they won the war. The temple was then rededicated. Hence, the span of 1,260 days (or three and a half years, or time, times, and half a time, or forty-two months)—became a symbol in Jewish consciousness of a period of time when one faces great suffering and struggle, but with the assurance that God will triumph in the end.

So it is here in Revelation 12. John is speaking of the church—of you and me. We are in that time of suffering and struggle. We are living through a compressed time, a concentrated time. This time will be cut short for the sake of the elect, but there will be persecution and opposition and antagonism from this beast until the consummation takes place.

Now, let us look at verses 7–9:

Now war arose in heaven, Michael and his angels fighting against the dragon. And the dragon and his angels fought back, but he was defeated and there was no longer any place for them in heaven. And the great dragon was thrown down, that ancient serpent, who is called the devil and Satan, the deceiver of the whole world—he was thrown down to the earth, and his angels were thrown down with him.

27

Here also we find, again in highly symbolic language, the struggle that takes place in heaven. What happens down here has its counterpart in heaven. The devil himself has now been defeated in the light of Christ's death and resurrection. He has been thrown out of heaven. He can no longer stand before God as the accuser of the brothers and sisters. How could he stand before God in this way? After all, these brethren have now been justified, vindicated by Christ's own death. Hurrying on to verse 10, we read of the salvation and the power in the kingdom of our God. We see the authority of the Messiah, who has thrown down the accuser of our brothers and sisters. How they triumph over this one is described in verse 11. Now look at verse 12: "Therefore, rejoice, O heavens and you who dwell in them! But woe to you, O earth and sea, for the devil has come down to you in great wrath, because he knows that his time is short!"

Having outlined the occasion for satanic rage, John in the second place identifies the reasons for this rage.

> But the woman was given the two wings of the great eagle so that she might fly from the serpent into the wilderness, to the place where she is to be nourished for a time, and times, and half a time. The serpent poured water like a river out of his mouth after the woman, to sweep her away with a flood. But the earth came to the help of the woman, and the earth opened its mouth and swallowed the river that the dragon had poured from his mouth. (Rev. 12:14-16)

There are several reasons for Satan's rage. First, the devil knows his time is short (vv. 10 and 12). Second, he knows that the fear he is able to induce is restricted. He has been cast out of heaven. He has no more access to God in the way, for example,

28

that he has access to God in the book of Job. Third, his success is limited. In verses 14–16, the ongoing conflict between Satan and the church is described.

Interestingly, there is a lot of exodus typology in these verses. The woman is given the wings of an eagle, which recalls Exodus 19 and Isaiah 40. The attempt to drown the people of God in a flood is reminiscent of the way Satan attempted to get rid of Moses. The opening of the earth brings to mind the judgment that fell in Numbers 16. All of these sorts of things are called to mind in this ongoing symbolism of aid and struggle. One remembers the words of Isaiah 43:2, "When you pass through the waters, I will be with you."

Now throughout the history of the church, Christians have frequently disagreed on whether things are getting better or getting worse. But allow me to be bold and tell you what's going to happen.

There is a wonderful parable reported in Matthew 13:24–30 about the wheat and the tares, or weeds. The disciples want to pull out the weeds that an enemy has sown in God's own field. The master simply replies, "No, let both grow until the end." In the last two thousand years, there have been conversions to Christ—and there have been murders. This is, in part, what Jesus means when he says, "Let both grow to the end." Furthermore, if the Lord Jesus doesn't come back for another one or two hundred years, let me tell you what will happen: there will be spectacular times of gospel growth that will be hugely encouraging, and millions and millions of people will be converted. Bibles will be printed, and preachers and teachers will arise, and the whole society will be changed. Culture will be transformed by the preaching of the gospel.

But there will also be persecution and violence and antagonism. This is what Jesus means when he says, "Let both grow until the end." And this is exactly what we see here in the book Revelation as well. Christ has risen. Christ is triumphant. Satan is already a defeated foe; he is gone, banished from heaven. His fear is restricted, and he knows his time is short. This is precisely why he is filled with fury.

This reminds me of one of the momentous events of World War II. In June 1944, the Russians were pushing the Germans back in the east. The Western Allies had already cleaned out North Africa. They had made a little foray into southern France and were pushing up the boot of Italy as well. They were holding their own in the Balkans.

But then in June 1944, in three days on the beaches of Normandy, the Western Allies dumped over one million men and many tons of war material. Anybody who had a brain in his head could see that the war had been decided; in terms of manpower, productive capacity, energy supply, technological efficiency, perseverance, and money, it was simply over. All that the Germans had going for them was the fact that at least Germany had not yet been invaded.

So did Hitler give up and sue for peace? Not at all. Instead, some of the bloodiest fighting of the war was still to come. In the Battle of the Bulge, the Germans pushed toward the coast—and would have made it if they hadn't run out of fuel. Then there was the battle for Berlin, which was perhaps more bloody than any other. Why did these things happen? Because Hitler was filled with fury.

The same goes for Satan today. He is filled with fury, not because he thinks he can win, but precisely because he knows he cannot. He is filled with fury because he knows his time is short, and so his malice runs deep against God and all of God's people. Locked out of heaven, locked even out of his ancient function as the accuser of the brothers and sisters, Satan rages.

This ought to be a huge part of how we think about this evil age. Of course, there are many other facets to it. It is possible to talk about the ongoing presence of God manifested in creation. It is possible to talk about the goodness of God and the streams of common grace in the arts and sciences. It is possible to talk about the way, even before we are Christians, that we are human beings made in the image of God. There are many things that we enjoy, and one does not want to paint a simply negative picture, in which there is nothing but antagonism. It is much more complicated and subtle than that, to be sure.

Satan himself is sometimes portrayed as a roaring lion, seeking whom he may devour (1 Peter 5:8). At other times, he is portrayed as an angel of light, deceiving the very elect, if that were possible (2 Cor. 11:14). So sometimes he may be unleashing his arsenal so as to cause the deaths of a multitude of believers, as recently has happened in Sudan. At other times, he may be sending out false teaching that very subtly undermines the truth. He will not come right out and say, "Look! Here is a load of false teaching!" He is not stupid. He is going to say, "Oh, I think it's wonderful that you believe the gospel. The gospel is such a good thing—isn't God nice? But, you know, we have discovered something that helps you to apply the gospel to your life just a little better. In addition to believing the gospel, you need these extra techniques in your counseling. This will be hugely helpful for those of you who have come from an abusive background." He will suggest things like that. He will constantly tempt us to multiply things, and multiply things, and multiply things until the gospel is made essentially irrelevant because it becomes that which is merely assumed. It is not what you are excited about anymore. It's not at the forefront of your thinking.

Gospel Sufficiency

I have been teaching for more decades now than I can count, and if I have learned anything from all of this teaching, it's this: my students don't learn everything I teach them; what they learn is what I'm excited about. So within the church of the living God, we must become excited about the gospel. That's how we pass on our heritage. If, instead, the gospel increasingly becomes for us that which we assume, then we will, of course, assent to the correct creedal statement. But, at this point, the gospel is not what really captures us. Rather, it is a particular form of worship, or a particular style of counseling, or a particular view of culture, or a particular technique in preaching, or—fill in the blank. Then, ultimately, our students make that their center, and the generation after us loses the gospel. As soon as you get to the place where the gospel is that which is nearly assumed, you are only a generation and a half from death.

So now, let me take just a moment to show you that the picture I have given here in apocalyptic categories from the book of Revelation is, in fact, assumed throughout the New Testament. I will do this merely by pointing to one book very quickly. Galatians is about as nonapocalyptic a book as you can imagine. However, I want to insist strongly that, although the language in Revelation 12 is certainly apocalyptic, the stance itself is very common. Let us look, briefly, at what I mean from the book of Galatians.

We begin in Galatians 1. There the apostle Paul tells us that he was sent, not with a human commission or by human authority, but by Jesus Christ and God the Father, who raised him from the dead. Look at what he then says in verses 3–5:

Grace to you and peace from God our Father and the Lord Jesus Christ, who gave himself for our sins to deliver us from the present evil age, according to the will of our God and Father, to whom be the glory forever and ever. Amen.

Paul is here describing the start of the conflict we have been speaking of. The rescue turns on Christ sacrificing himself for our sins. So the rescue is from the guilt and the power of sin. This happens in this present evil age according to the will of God our Father, to whom be the glory forever and ever. That's the introduction.

Then, in verses 6–9, Paul identifies those who oppose gospel exclusiveness. What characterizes this present evil age, amongst other things, is that which denies gospel exclusiveness. Paul speaks in the strongest possible language in verses 8 and 9:

> But even if we or an angel from heaven should preach to you a gospel contrary to the one we preached to you, let him be accursed. As we have said before, so now I say again: If anyone is preaching to you a gospel contrary to the one you received, let him be accursed.

In 2:1–5, Paul identifies the opponents of gospel sufficiency. In this case, Titus, a Gentile lad, was brought to Jerusalem. Paul insisted that he did not have to be circumcised to be accepted by the Christian leaders in Jerusalem. Here was the reason: if you can only be acceptable to Christians in Jerusalem because you have the gospel plus circumcision, then the gospel itself is not enough. Yet there were "false brothers" in the church who demanded that he be circumcised. This was a threat to gospel sufficiency, which is a part of this present evil age.

Paul continues in 2:11–21. He wants us to know about opponents to the truth of the gospel in exclusive justification, which space prohibits me from unpacking further. In chapters 3 and 4, we see opponents to biblical cohesiveness. The whole argument of these chapters is Paul saying to the Galatians, "Don't you understand that this gospel that I am preaching was announced in the Old Testament?" In 5:1–6, we see opponents to gospel freedom and grace. Beginning in verse 7, the apostle speaks of opponents to gospel perseverance. These people were never really committed to the gospel. In verse 13 and following, Paul shows us opponents to gospel fruitfulness. This section, of course, contains the well-known detailing of the fruit of the Spirit. We are reminded that the gospel is more than justification. Justification declares our standing before God. But the gospel is also the wonderful news of what God has done by pouring out his Spirit, causing us to be regenerated and then transformed. Thus the principle Jesus announced—"By their fruits you shall know them"—remains true in the apostle's vision of the Christian life.

It is not merely a matter of believing the right things. Genuine faith leads to the bearing of good fruit. The gospel is the announcement of the powerful thing that God has done. The gospel transforms us and separates us from this present evil age. It makes us different.

Christians Overcoming

This leads me to conclude with the verse we skipped in Revelation 12. It is right to think about the characteristics and profile of this present evil age. It is right to think of the place of the devil, as he maliciously controls these structures, mustering opposition and violence against God's people. It is right to think of all these things, but Revelation 12:11 tells us how Christians overcome the devil: "And they have conquered him by the blood of the Lamb and by the word of their testimony, for they loved not their lives even unto death."

Now, this deserves a couple of sermons just by itself, but let me briefly outline the three points that John makes. First, Christians overcome satanic rage by the blood of the Lamb. In fact, the original language is even stronger; it says that Christians overcome Satan quite literally "on the ground of the blood of the Lamb." So it is not by the blood of the Lamb seen as a kind of device, but it is on the ground of Christ's atoning death. Satan comes to accuse us psychologically or tries to vent his voice before God, saying, "How can you let that Don Carson walk away? He is a sinner, for goodness sake! You claim to be so holy, God, yet you let him go free." What do we say? My plea is not, "I am not as bad as all that." My plea is the blood of the Lamb—that is what silences the accusations. This is gospel freedom and this is why Satan has been cast out. The cross stands at the heart of everything. This needs to be unpacked and teased out again and again and again, so we understand the riches of what we have in Christ in overcoming Satan and all of his wiles.

Second, Christians overcome by the word of their testimony. That does not mean that they give their testimonies frequently. This refers to the word of their *witness*; that is, they bear witness to the gospel. How are we going to advance the gospel? How are we going to push back the frontiers of darkness in America today? Some people advise us to start a political party. Maybe we should do some lobbying in Washington. There may be some place for these kinds of things as part of God's common grace, but they should not be confused with gospel-centeredness.

John is telling us that the hosts of darkness are pushed back by Christians bearing witness—giving testimony to who God is and what he has done in Christ Jesus. How else can we push back against Satan and his forces? We will be defeated if we simply keep silent. If you never share the gospel with anybody else, you yourself are defeated. You are not pushing back the frontiers of darkness. This is how Satan is defeated—by the blood of the Lamb and by the word of your testimony.

Third, Satan is overcome when we do not shrink back, even from death itself. We are called to die daily. This is what it means to follow a Savior who went to the cross. We are to learn afresh to take up our crosses and follow him. This is why Paul could write things like this: "For it has been granted to you that for the sake of Christ you should not only believe in him but also suffer for his sake" (Phil. 1:29). This has been *granted* to us. Or think of that remarkable passage, Acts 5:41, when the apostles were first beaten for proclaiming the gospel. What did they do? Luke tells us that they rejoiced "that they were counted worthy to suffer dishonor for the name."

Recently I began to understand why the apostles rejoiced on this occasion. After all, before Jesus went to the cross, he spent a fair bit of what we call the "Farewell Discourse" talking about how his own followers would suffer. He had done so earlier in Matthew 10. He anticipated this in Matthew 5:10: "Blessed are those who are persecuted for righteousness' sake, for theirs is the kingdom of heaven." Then again in verse 12: "Rejoice and be glad, for your reward is great in heaven, for so they persecuted the prophets who were before you."

Now, in Acts 5, Jesus has gone back to heaven, the Spirit has fallen, and Pentecostal power is causing many people to be converted. I imagine that if the apostles were thoughtful at all, they were sometimes saying to themselves, "This is fantastic, but where is the suffering?" Then it happens; they are beaten, and what do they say? "At last!" That is stunning.

Now, if we truly understand that this is how Christians ought to react in this fallen world, it changes everything. You too will rejoice that you were counted worthy to suffer for the name. This suffering will take different forms for each of us.

Some of us will be called to suffer intellectually. We will be mocked for taking up our cross and daily following Jesus with our minds. For others, it will be actual physical suffering that we have to endure. I look at my brothers and sisters who suffer horrible physical torments, and then I witness how they adorn the blessed gospel with forbearing perseverance. I watch them forgive their tormentors. Still I wonder why salvation should cause them so much pain.

But then I recall our Savior's words: "Remember the word that I said to you: 'A servant is not greater than his master.' If they persecuted me, they will also persecute you" (John 15:20). And so Satan will be overcome as we remember these words of our Lord and, remembering them, practice them in our daily lives. These three things from Revelation 12 are God's ordained means of overcoming our enemy and living to the glory of our Savior in this present evil age.

3

The Age of The Spirit

ALISTAIR BEGG

*Being therefore exalted at the right hand of God,
and having received from the Father the promise
of the Holy Spirit, he has poured out this that you
yourselves are seeing and hearing. (Acts 2:33)*

ONE OF THE GREAT MYSTERIES, when studying
the New Testament, is how we come to terms with the dramatic
transformation that takes place in a relatively short period of
time. Between the events on the evening of Christ's death and
the events described for us in Acts 2:32–33, we see why this
was the case.

Before we look at Acts 2, we need to look back at Luke 24.
The gospel of Luke is the first volume of a two-volume work;
Acts is, we could say, volume 2. Here in Luke 24:13–32 we meet

two disconsolate disciples making their way along the road. They meet a stranger, who asks a strange question: what's going on around here? Well, you know what happens: they give voice to the fact that their hopes and expectations came to a crashing end three days earlier, as Jesus was crucified. By the time you get to verse 31, however, their hopes are revived. This happens because of Jesus' intervention. He opens their eyes and their hearts to understand the Scriptures. Case closed, right? Not exactly, for in verse 37 he appears again and the same disciples are startled again, thinking Jesus to be a ghost. So they haven't exactly put everything together.

The Spirit from Christ's Ascension

As we turn forward to the book of Acts, it becomes clear in chapter 1 why these disciples only partly understood things—they had more to learn. So in Acts 1:3 we read this concerning Jesus: "To them he presented himself alive after his suffering by many proofs, appearing to them during forty days and speaking about the kingdom of God." Jesus did not ascend directly to heaven after his resurrection; he stayed for a period of forty days to teach them and to answer their questions. All of this was to prepare them for the coming of the Holy Spirit. It is the ascension of Christ, then, which prepares for the outpouring of the Holy Spirit.

When some people preach, especially if they preach a certain view of Pentecost and its ongoing impact in the life of the Christian, they suggest that the disciples themselves were the key to Pentecost. It is suggested that they got themselves in the right kind of position or mood and then God responded, giving them the Holy Spirit. Nothing could be further from the truth. It was the ascension of Christ that gave rise to the pouring out of gifts, as Paul will later tell us in Ephesians 4.

So it's important for us to recognize that the story does not end simply with a resurrected Christ, but with an ascended Lord and King. The expectations of these early disciples, like ours, were flawed. That is why the question they ask in Acts 1:6 is so significant: "So when they had come together, they asked him, 'Lord, will you at this time restore the kingdom to Israel?'"

Now, this is actually the wrong question. It is wrong chronologically, and it is wrong geographically. It is surely understandable, but it's wrong. Jesus' answer to this question establishes for them—and for us—the way in which the kingdom of God comes. It establishes for them the significance of what we are referring to as "the age of the Spirit." The short answer Jesus gives them is that the kingdom comes through the preaching of the gospel, by the power of the Holy Spirit. His answer, perhaps, helped them understand what Jesus had said in John 16:7: "Nevertheless, I tell you the truth: it is to your advantage that I go away." How hard it must have been for them to understand that! But now they are beginning to discover just exactly what it was that Jesus had been saying. Any remaining lack of clarity in their minds was resolved in the giving of the Spirit on the day of Pentecost.

But here in verse 6 of chapter 1, we see that their expectations were fairly straightforward for Jewish people. They thought that the kingdom would appear and be established in Jerusalem. The Gentiles would then be overturned, and the temple would be put in its proper position of prominence. The kingdom would appear as a political reality, with Jerusalem and the temple at its center.

Now, ironically, I have discovered that this is actually not an uncommon perspective here in America, as you listen to

Christian people talking about the future of the world. The Jews thought that Jerusalem was the center of the world, and some Christians here in our country seem to think that as goes Washington, D.C., so goes the world.

But this is all wrong, just like those ancient disciples' thinking. Instead, Jesus explains to them that his scepter is going to rule in and beyond and through Jerusalem to the ends of the earth. How? By the preached word, using the missionary endeavor of God's people throughout the entire earth. Again, it is at the ascension that all of this begins to fall into line, because it is in the ascension that the work of Christ is completed, proving God's full acceptance of Christ's sacrifice.

The Spirit in Peter's Preaching

What happens when the Holy Spirit is first poured out? First and foremost, there is the reversal of the curse of Babel. This happens as Jesus' Galilean disciples are speaking in other tongues. And it should not escape our attention that the first impact of the outpouring of the Holy Spirit is the powerful preaching of Peter. The first dramatic impact, if you like, of the age of the Spirit being ushered forth in this way is a sermon. It may seem self-serving for a preacher to point this out, but you can determine whether what I am saying is accurate or not.

Peter preaches in such a way as to declare Jesus to be Lord, the ruler of history and the Savior of his people (Acts 2:32–36). As we think about this, we must recognize that Pentecost has to be seen in light of all the work of Jesus. It has to be seen in terms of Christ's life of obedience, his atoning death, the reality of his resurrection, and so on. All of these things are unrepeatable. Jesus' resurrection is unrepeatable. His ascension is unrepeatable. And Pentecost is unrepeatable. These are all unique events.

Now, you may say, "Well, it's not really a unique event, insofar as the Spirit was present in the Old Testament, prior to the outpouring that we see here in Acts 2." Yes, in that sense it is not unique. But it is unique insofar as the Spirit comes to minister with respect to the gospel event that has been fulfilled in Christ's death and resurrection. I like John Murray's pithy saying that Pentecost is not an event to be repeated, but neither is it an event to be retracted. It has an abiding effect, an abiding significance for the fulfillment of God's saving design.

Pentecost has three implications for the ministry of the gospel and our experience as Christians. First of all, it is important for the content of our preaching—what we are supposed to be preaching about. I have the great privilege and responsibility of being a teacher of the Bible. It is good for those of us who preach and teach to think about our content. But it is also good for those who are normally listeners to be reminded of what it is that we're supposed to be doing.

In John 16:12, Jesus says, "I still have many things to say to you, but you cannot bear them now." He is telling his disciples that they are not going to get into the whole business this evening, so to speak. Jesus continues, however, in verses 13–15:

> When the Spirit of truth comes, he will guide you into all the truth, for he will not speak on his own authority, but whatever he hears he will speak, and he will declare to you the things that are to come. He will glorify me, for he will take what is mine and declare it to you. All that the Father has is mine; therefore I said that he will take what is mine and declare it to you.

These verses are often wrested to the destruction of the reader, I must admit. But what we realize, if we read them properly and look at them carefully, is that the truth that Jesus promises to the apostles, which is given to them, is ours in the Scriptures. This is the truth into which he brings or will bring his followers. It is that which has been inscripturated. Thus, what we have to proclaim is all the truth respecting Jesus that is given to us: his life, his word, his work, and so on. All of it is deposited for us in the apostolic witness. So Jesus is not suggesting that we all sit around and try to discover truth for ourselves. He is making an express promise to his apostles, on this occasion, to be fulfilled in the giving of his Spirit.

Now, we can test this to see just exactly how it worked out. And, as I have already pointed out, the first impact of the giving of the Spirit is the preaching of Peter. Therefore, let's look at the preaching of Peter, albeit briefly, to see whether what Jesus has promised here in the gospel of John is now being fulfilled.

In Acts 2, Peter begins to preach. And what does he do? He stands up with the eleven and tells the people that the men they have heard speaking in tongues are not drunk, as the people think, for it is only 9:00 in the morning (v. 14). Rather, this is what was spoken by the prophet Joel. Here he takes the Bible and brings it to bear upon the circumstances, circumstances about which he himself has been so phenomenally confused. And, as we read Acts 2, we discover that Jesus is the center and the substance of Peter's preaching.

Jesus has told us that the work of the Spirit of God is to take all the riches he has from the Father and give them out in such a way that his disciples will be enabled to go to the ends of the earth and proclaim the reality of all this. And Peter stands up and does exactly that.

Sometimes, when I go back to Glasgow, I notice buildings that I didn't notice when I was there before. This is partly because a lot of them have been or are being cleaned since I was there as a boy. But it also has to do with lighting. All of a sudden, when you are driving through a part of the west end of Glasgow, you notice a building for the first time because it is now being floodlit, and the floodlights have made all of the difference. Suddenly that which has been obscure is now noticeable.

That's what we have here in Peter's sermon in Acts 2: it is the floodlighting ministry of the Holy Spirit. The ministry of the Holy Spirit is, if you like, to floodlight the Lord Jesus Christ. That is the implication of the Spirit being poured out upon his people.

So Peter stands up and speaks about "Jesus of Nazareth, a man attested to you by God with mighty works and wonders and signs that God did through him in your midst, as you yourselves know" (v. 22). Now we shouldn't make too much of how Peter speaks about Jesus, calling him "Jesus of Nazareth." But we shouldn't overlook it, either. It is, I think, a perfect way to speak of both the humanity and the deity of Christ. He was fully man: "Jesus of Nazareth, a man." But he was also fully God: "attested to you by God with mighty works and wonders and signs."

This is so different from much modern preaching. Peter could have been like most modern preachers, standing up and saying, "Ladies and gentlemen, I am glad you are here this morning! I am delighted to have the opportunity to talk to you. I want to tell you how I was trying to contextualize myself in relationship to something that I saw the other day on CNN." You know how it goes. And after about fifteen minutes, you say to yourself, "Is there any Jesus in this at all?"

You would never have thought this about Peter's preaching. Why? Because the work of the Spirit is to floodlight Jesus. Peter continues in verse 23, telling the crowd about who Jesus is: he is the Savior provided by God. I know he says, in effect, that there is a lot of talk going around Jerusalem about Jesus' death. Was it the work of the Romans? Was it the work of the Jewish leaders? Who did it? What does Peter say? He declares that Jesus' death happened according to God's set purpose and foreknowledge, but that his listeners, with the help of wicked men, put him to death, nailing him to a cross. Who is going to be brave enough to stand in the middle of Jerusalem and say such a thing? How can anyone make such a declaration, but by the enabling power of the Holy Spirit?

In verse 24, Peter continues to tell us what our content for preaching is. He says, "God raised him up, loosing the pangs of death, because it was not possible for him to be held by it." Peter tells us that Jesus is the exalted Lord. He is saying, "You think I'm crazy, but I will tell you what, Jesus is alive, and Jesus is the ascended King. Jesus has fulfilled his promises, and I am here to tell you about it." Again, what does he preach from? He simply preaches the Bible. He preaches from Psalm 16. He speaks of David seeing Yahweh, the covenant Lord, but Peter says that he was seeing Jesus, for Jesus is the covenant Lord.

Now don't miss this: if one of the implications of living in the age of the Spirit is the preaching of God's word, then we must ensure that it is Christ we preach. Further, we must make sure that the Christ we preach is the Christ of the Scriptures.

There are a lot of people talking about Jesus today, but they are not necessarily teaching Jesus as he is revealed in the Bible. It is a Jesus of their own making. It is a designer Jesus that they preach, trimmed to the needs and aspirations and hopes and predilections of a group that they have no interest in offending, but simply wooing. This is not at all what Peter did—or what we should do, for that matter. You will also notice that it is the Spirit of God and the word of God working together. Years ago,

I heard a little trilogy, and I think it still has validity. It went: "All word and no Spirit and the people dry up. All Spirit and no word and the people blow up. But both Spirit and word and the people grow up."

The Spirit in the Missionary Church

The second implication of living in the age of the Spirit is that it affects our fulfillment of the Great Commission. What we have discovered so far is simply this: the Great Commission is going to be fulfilled only by the power of the Holy Spirit, through the proclamation of the gospel. Remember, from the disciples' question in chapter 1, that they were still thinking in terms of Jerusalem, thinking in terms of a temple being rebuilt. But they were going to have to realize that they needed to get out of Jerusalem and go to the nations. How the disciples must have yearned to see a literal rebuilt temple, with the best congregation the world had ever seen!

What does Jesus tell them? He says, "Actually, that's not going to happen." Surely they wanted to ask him, "Why not?" Jesus essentially tells them, "Because you are going to go out into another world. That's why I want you to wait until you receive the power of the Holy Spirit, so that you might do what the Spirit has been given to you to do." Jesus is going to leave them physically, but he is going to be present with them by his Spirit. He is going to send them out to the ends of the earth. Why? Because the church is a missionary church.

We read in Revelation 5:9 that Jesus has "ransomed people for God from every tribe and language and people and nation." How is there going to be a company that no one can number, from every tribe, nation, people, and language gathered around the throne, declaring that salvation belongs to the Lord? How is that going to be achieved? We know it is by divine appointment. But that doesn't mean that the gathering happens by itself. There is still a strain of thought in some of our circles that goes all the way back to the days of William Carey. Remember what they said to him? "Sit down, Mr. Carey. If God wants to evangelize India, he will do it fine without you." And then they put their top hats back on and went out, muttering, "Silly man!" But the company we read about here is gathered by means of the proclamation of the gospel. God ordains men and women to salvation, but he also ordains the means whereby they come to salvation. That's what Jesus wants these disciples to see. "You are not going to stay here," he says. "You are going to go out."

Missionary zeal is in decline in the circles in which I move, sad to say. I just came back from South America, and their enrollment is significantly down across the board. Young people, teenagers, and university students now regard four years as a lifetime of service. Full-time missionary service has now been truncated to four years. Short-term mission trips are now a quick flight from Miami to San Juan and back again on Tuesday and—Presto!—you can put that on your résumé. You haven't done anything apart from taking some miserable photographs and expending a bit of time and money.

I simply want to point out that the world missionary endeavor, from the United Kingdom and from the United States, is declining. We are a long way removed from "He is no fool, who gives up what he cannot keep to gain what he cannot lose." We are largely removed from "Lord, give me Scotland or I die!" What has changed?

We no longer believe in the age of the Spirit. Thus, it is no longer the age of the missionary church. It is no longer our desire to answer the call of God and go to the ends of the earth, losing ourselves (joyfully) in his service. When was the last time you heard anybody singing hymns like "So Send I You," by Margaret Clarkson?[1] When was the last time your church sang, as Clarkson writes, about being sent out to labor for God with no immediate earthly reward—without pay, without love, without being sought out or known? Words like these from hymns like that are neither spoken nor sung today because we have lost our missionary zeal. And young people are growing up with the bizarre notion that somehow other people will take care of it. If I could say just one thing to you, if you're a young person wondering what in the world to do with your life, this is it: Give up your small ambitions. Recognize that this is still the age of the Spirit, and be willing to be sent by Christ to carry this amazing news to the ends of the earth.

The Spirit in Personal Appropriation

The third and final implication of this being the age of the Spirit has to do with our own personal appropriation of the Holy Spirit. Once again, it is not unusual in the circles in which I move to listen to people describe the distinctive way in which the Spirit of God came to these initial disciples. They make it so remote, so unusual, so out there, that we manage to sidestep any implication of our personal appropriation of the Spirit of God.

Read the Upper Room Discourse again. John 14:23 says, "If anyone loves me, he will keep my word, and my Father will love him, and we will come to him and make our home with him." We want

1. "So Send I You." Lyrics: Margaret Clarkson, 1954. Music: John W. Peterson, 1954.

to ask, "How are you going to do that, Jesus?" He might answer us, "In a remarkable number of ways, actually." He might tell us that it will happen in the glory of the preached Word, or in the reality of corporate prayers, or in our own personal walk with God.

Think about it in relationship, again, to the preacher and then to those in the pews. A word to pastors: are we just going to read this, or are we going to ask God to make it real in our own preaching? Remember Paul's words: "Our gospel came to you not only in word, but also in power and in the Holy Spirit and with full conviction" (1 Thess. 1:5). Paul brought them information, to be sure—it was true, it was historical data, it was factual material—but when it came to these Thessalonians, it did not come like a long, boring lecture! Fellow preachers, our people's faith needs to rest not in our power, but in God's power. If we understand the Bible at all, we know that God puts this treasure in earthen vessels or clay pots, so that the transcendent power might be seen to belong to him and not to us. So we need to get alone in our studies and ask God to give us all that he has for us. You must do this, if you preach God's word. We must realize that God is more willing to bless us and enrich us than we are even to take the time to ask him. And because we do not know how to do this, it is no wonder that so many of our sermons sound the way they do.

Finally, how does this personal appropriation apply to those of you in the pews? If you want to see effective Bible teaching and preaching Sunday after Sunday, you need at least two things: first, you need a praying pastor, and second, you need a praying congregation. You will be surprised at what happens if you just pray for your pastor while he is preaching. Pray for him before he preaches, and pray for him after he preaches. You will discover that he is preaching the most unbelievable sermons you have ever heard in your entire life. They will be the same sermons, but they will be experienced in an entirely different way.

So when you get in the pew, say, "Lord, turn this lecture that I am hearing into something from you yourself. Do something in the man, please." This reminds me of what the late Professor John Murray used to do. He would have people drive him to the airport or wherever, and he would ask trick questions. On one occasion, he asked his traveling friend, "What is the difference between a lecture and preaching?" His friend tried and tried, but could not answer it in the way that Murray wanted. (Few people could answer Murray's questions with the precision he demanded!) Here was Murray's answer: "Preaching is a personal, passionate plea." And as you sit in the pew week by week, you must ask God to make the lecture into a personal, passionate plea.

But you must also appropriate the Spirit in how you live day by day. This means that you look to Jesus for pardon and for power. He will give you both, through his Spirit. You will begin to see that power at work in your life, day by day. You will begin to see things change, simply by appropriating personally what the Holy Spirit has promised in his Word.

So if this is the age of the Spirit—and it is—and if God has poured out his Spirit on his disciples in a definitive way—and he has—then, there is absolutely no reason why we should not be crying out to God. We must cry out to him to revive his work in the midst of the years, to show himself strong, and to turn the floodlights on his Son, the Lord Jesus Christ, so that he might see of the travail of his soul and be satisfied. All that we do is worth nothing unless God blesses our labors. Therefore, pray the words of the old hymn:

> Come down, O love divine, seek Thou this soul of mine,
> And visit it with Thine own ardor glowing.
> O Comforter, draw near, within my heart appear,
> And kindle it, Thy holy flame bestowing.[2]

2. Bianco of Siena, "Come Down, O Love Divine," c. 1434.

4

The Resurrection Hope

MICHAEL S. HORTON

But in fact Christ has been raised from the dead,
the firstfruits of those who have fallen asleep.
(1 Corinthians 15:20)

THE RESURRECTION is our hope. It is not just something that shapes the way we anticipate the future. It really is an indicator of what we believe about everything—what we believe about God and his relationship to the world, what we believe about creation, providence, and redemption. Getting the resurrection right is essential for understanding everything in Scripture, from promise to fulfillment.

What is your ultimate hope? Let me give you three options. First, is your ultimate hope that you will go to heaven when you die, finally liberated from this world and everything physical—

53

just being a soul in the presence of God? Second, is your ultimate hope making the world a better place, maybe having your best life now, or the best world now? This option can be understood in individualistic terms or more sociocultural terms. Or, third, is your ultimate hope that of the resurrection of the body and the life everlasting?

The answer to those questions should be pretty easy because the third option is what we confess in our creeds. We believe ultimately in the resurrection of the body, the resurrection of the dead, and the life everlasting. But this hope didn't start with us as Christians.

A Jewish-Christian Hope

This hope is something that the Jews were looking forward to as well. At least the Pharisees were. Does that surprise you? In Jesus' day, the Pharisees were faithfully interpreting the prophets (at this point, at least) when they looked forward to that day when they would individually participate in a cosmic regeneration. They divided history into this present age, under sin and death, and the age to come, which would be dominated by life and righteousness. The Pharisees looked forward to the resurrection of the just at the end of the age.

This is one of the reasons why John the Baptist got a little bit impatient and frustrated with Jesus. He sent his disciples to ask Jesus, "Are you the one who is to come, or shall we look for another?" (Luke 7:20). John evidently expected the resurrection of the just to happen in his lifetime—and he was waiting to be beheaded!

So there was a great expectation that all of these things would be accomplished when the Messiah came. But Jesus himself thought that they would be accomplished in not one, but two comings. When he came the first time, it was to accomplish salvation; when he comes the next time, it will be to consummate his reign (cf. Heb. 9:28).

Now the Christians of the first century (and afterwards, really) were in a different milieu as well. The more they reached out to Gentiles, the more this gospel had to be communicated to people who didn't get that story at all. They weren't looking for the resurrection of the body—they were looking for *escape* from the body.

The great systems of Greek philosophy taught that matter was evil. They said that humans were eternal souls imprisoned in material bodies. So the goal of salvation in Greek thought was to ascend through intellectual contemplation and spiritual meditation, to rise above the level of history, matter, and nature to the transcendent world of eternal, unchanging truths.

We see much the same thing today. Every Easter we are treated to cover stories in periodicals like *Time* and *Newsweek*. While they are usually just blatant attacks on this or that doctrine of Christianity, occasionally they provide insight into where our culture is going on some of these issues. During one of these Easter publishing flurries, Lisa Miller wrote a very interesting article in *Newsweek* indicating that, while 80 percent of Americans claim they believe in heaven, few of us have the slightest clue about what this means. Almost everyone surveyed agreed that heaven is the good place you go after death, usually as a reward for a struggle, or for being faithful, or for being a good person. But then confusion enters in. On the one hand, many people talked about meeting up with loved ones and picking up where they left off on earth. On the other hand, people think of heaven as an ethereal place where we drift around, adrift from our bodies (pardon the pun). It seems to me, however, that a body was pretty crucial to hanging out with grandma and spouses and children back on earth! And Miller asks the logical question: if you don't have a body in heaven, what kind of heaven are you hoping for? She further points out that Americans now favor reincarnation over resurrection by 10 percent. Thirty percent of Americans believe in reincarnation, and 20 percent believe in resurrection.

Now here is where it gets shocking (but maybe it shouldn't): 21 percent of professing Christians believe in reincarnation over resurrection! This is due, at least in part, I think, to the fact that it is hard to die in America. We don't even use the language of death anymore. We speak of "passing away." Such language came into our vocabulary from Mary Baker Eddy, the founder of Christian Science. She denied the reality of evil and of matter, and therefore said that a person must rise above matter, so to speak. One needs only to believe that matter is an illusion. Evil is an illusion. Just believe this, and evil will go away.

According to her, the same holds for death: don't believe in it. You don't really die; you just pass away. And now we hear this in Christian circles. But "passing away" is very different from dying. More troubling is the fact that there is no resurrection for people who pass away.

My point with all of this is that, just like the ancient Christians in a pagan culture, we struggle in our culture between these two poles: the longing of the Jews for the resurrection and the Greek belief that matter is evil. We yearn for the restored cosmos that God made. We look forward to the day when there will no longer be a distinction between the temple in Jerusalem and the whole earth, when there will be no vertical distinction between heaven and earth. We look for the day when God will make his dwelling among his people.

But then we struggle, because this is such a different mindset when contrasted with the Greek speculation that matter is inherently evil. This same attitude, as we've seen, is with us today. We struggle with a culture that says, "Can't wait to slip off the bonds of this mortal coil, get away, and fly out of this body!"

1 Corinthians and the Resurrection

Perhaps the best place to turn for wisdom in dealing with this struggle over the resurrection is 1 Corinthians 15. The early Christians in Corinth, like us, were struggling with how to deal with this disconnect between their Greek heritage and the Christian proclamation of the gospel. If we look at an article like Lisa Miller's in *Newsweek*, and then turn to what Paul is writing in 1 Corinthians 15:1–12, we see that the great apostle was dealing with many of the same questions from a culture very similar to ours. Here's what he says:

> Now I would remind you, brothers, of the gospel I preached to you, which you received, in which you stand, and by which you are being saved, if you hold fast to the word I preached to you—unless you believed in vain. For I delivered to you as of first importance what I also received: that Christ died for our sins in accordance with the Scriptures, that he was buried, that he was raised on the third day in accordance with the Scriptures, and that he appeared to Cephas, then to the twelve. Then he appeared to more than five hundred brothers at one time, most of whom are still alive, though some have fallen asleep. Then he appeared to James, then to all the apostles. Last of all, as to one untimely born, he appeared also to me. For I am the least of the apostles, unworthy to be called an apostle, because I persecuted the church of God. But by the grace of God I am

what I am, and his grace toward me was not in vain. On the contrary, I worked harder than any of them, though it was not I, but the grace of God that is with me. Whether then it was I or they, so we preach and so you believed. Now if Christ is proclaimed as raised from the dead, how can some of you say that there is no resurrection of the dead?

Paul begins with the fact of the resurrection. You don't start out with a philosophy; you don't start out with a scheme, as Greek philosophy did. No, Paul starts out with the fact of the resurrection of Christ. For him, the facts of the case may change your worldview. This particular event might actually destroy your expectations. It might surprise you a little bit, as to what you should expect at the end of the age.

So Paul was responding to questions the Corinthians themselves had asked him. We know this is so because he writes in 7:1, "Now concerning the matters about which you wrote." Then he proceeds to answer some of the Corinthians' questions. He tells them that sex is okay within marriage. The fact that this question was asked should alert us to the fact that we are again dealing with the Greek notion that matter is inherently evil.

Then in chapter 15, Paul addresses what is really the heart of the matter: the question of the resurrection of the body in the light of Jesus Christ's resurrection. Before I get into this in detail, however, I want to relate a story about a well-known Christian leader. One Easter, he was asked, in a nutshell, what is the purpose of life. He replied that life is preparation for eternity. "We were made to last forever, and God wants us to be with him in heaven. One day my heart is going to stop, and that will be the end of my body, but not the end of me." He said something along those lines. That is exactly the Greek worldview, rather than the biblical worldview.

What I hope to show, however, is that, while it is truly wonderful that the Lord takes our souls into his presence until the day of resurrection, our ultimate hope, as Paul argues here, is the resurrection hope. Strikingly, he says nothing less than that the gospel is at stake in all of this. Look at verses 1 and 2: "Now I would remind you, brothers, of the gospel I preached to you, which you received, in which you stand, and by which you are [present tense] being saved, if you hold fast to the word I preached to you—unless you believed in vain." What Paul is saying here is that the bodily resurrection of Jesus Christ is not an optional extra. He is arguing that Christianity may have all sorts of other redeeming qualities, but without this, nothing else matters.

Paul was writing only about twenty-five years after the event of Christ's resurrection itself. He could, at this early stage, go so far as to say that it was an established tradition. And this tradition that he received was that the tomb was empty, that Jesus was raised from the dead, and that he had then ascended to the right hand of the Father. Paul says that this is of "first importance." He very clearly tells us that what is most important in Christianity is the bodily resurrection of Jesus from the dead.

Now, remember who is writing this: Paul! He could have merely appealed to his eyewitness testimony on the Damascus Road. He could have said, "I had this great experience; I'm the last one who saw Jesus. I saw him at the right hand of the Father, and I heard his voice." But he doesn't even refer to his own firsthand encounter with the risen Christ. Instead, what he refers to are the Old Testament Scriptures as authoritatively anticipating this event. These Scriptures predicted that people would see this event unfold before their very eyes.

So, Paul says, the resurrection is not a legend, but something that eyewitnesses have been relating from the very beginning.

He goes on to tell us that on one occasion some five hundred people saw Jesus after he had been raised from the dead—"most of whom are still alive." "Go interview them if you want!" Paul seems to be saying. What other religion can do this? Could a Buddhist talk to people who saw Buddha rise from the dead? Do we find this in Islam? In these and every other religion, where are people who were contemporaries of a man who was supposedly raised from the dead told, "Go check the story with people who are alive"?

Paul's argument unfolds in verses 12–34. When you read through that section, notice how many times the apostle says that Christ "has been raised" from the dead. This phrase is in the Greek perfect tense, which is significant because this tense denotes something that has already been accomplished. Our Lord's resurrection has already been accomplished, Paul says. Then, when he refers to the general resurrection of the dead at the end of the age, he uses the present tense. Verse 16 says, "For if the dead are not raised, not even Christ has been raised." This is especially significant because Paul is already anticipating objections in his unfolding argument. If no one is raised from the dead, then Christ was not raised from the dead.

Verses 14–18 contain a number of different conclusions that Paul draws from the denial of the resurrection. First, Christ is not raised. Second, the preaching of the gospel is useless. As an aside, this should indicate to us how important is the historical nature of the gospel. According to Paul, the gospel is not "Let me tell you about my personal experience." To be sure, this may be included in our gospel presentation. But the gospel itself is not about what we've done or what we've experienced—otherwise we could just talk about that without the bodily resurrection of Jesus.

Continuing on, Paul says that, third, your faith is useless without Christ's resurrection. Furthermore, without the resurrection, fourth, Paul is bearing false witness and, fifth, you are still in your sins. Sixth, those who have already died are completely lost unless Christ has been raised. Finally, and in summary, Paul says that if we have hope in Christ in this life only, we of all men are most to be pitied.

From Paul's emphasis we learn that the gospel is not about having our best life now. It is not "Come to Christ and all of your problems will be solved." It is not an invitation to better marriages, better families, better health, greater wealth, or more personal fulfillment. It is not about finding meaning. It is not about social transformation. Again, all of these things may be the fruit of the gospel, but they are not the heart of the gospel!

Here is the gospel, according to Paul (and the rest of the biblical writers): God became flesh, fulfilled all righteousness, bore our curse, and rose triumphantly on the third day. That is the gospel. And Paul says that if these things didn't happen, people should feel sorry for us Christians.

Contrary to most people today, Paul was not a "spiritual" person, in the way that term is used today. Today a "spiritual" person is one who holds vague notions of all religions being the same and has really neat feelings while doing meditation or yoga. I don't think Paul would have gotten a call from the producers of Oprah. He really wasn't interested in spirituality. He was interested in things like bodies being raised. He was interested in the problem of death and saw the resurrection as the solution. Paul doesn't say, "Well, the family that prays together, stays together." He doesn't say, "Look at all the good effects on society if people believe in something." Former president Dwight Eisenhower said every country needs a religion, and he didn't care which one it was. Where I live in California, there is a bumper sticker that says, "You gotta believe in something; I believe I'll have another beer." What is this? It is faith in faith itself.

The apostle had nothing to do with anything even remotely close to this kind of thinking. He didn't have a sort of "running through the woods and meadows, singing joyfully with his hair flowing in the wind" kind of religion. Paul's religion was about the blood and gore of death. It was about the realities of dying and what happens after death, when the sovereign God who created us calls us to give an account for our lives. And so, if Christ isn't raised from the dead—if this is not historically accurate—then there is nothing redeeming about Christianity for Paul. If Christ has not risen bodily from the dead, then it doesn't matter what therapeutic benefits Christianity has had in your life. The net effect is that you have believed a hoax. It isn't useful, it isn't advantageous, and it hasn't made you a better person. It's a hoax; you have placed your faith in a lie.

So everything depends on Christ's bodily resurrection. Paul is betting all his chips on the historical, bodily resurrection of Jesus Christ. It is all for nothing if Jesus is still decaying in a tomb in Palestine today. There is no compensation for him living on in our hearts. What did the old hymn say, "You ask me how I know he lives? He lives within my heart." That is not the gospel. There is no hope if Jesus Christ's material body was not somehow reorganized and reenergized by the powers of the age to come and thus raised from the dead.

There was a German Marxist philosopher named Ernst Bloch who recognized this. He never became a Christian, but he said it wasn't the morality of the Sermon on the Mount that enabled Christianity to conquer Roman paganism (this was a popular argument in the early twentieth century). Rather, he argued, it was the belief that Jesus had been raised from the dead. In an age when Roman senators vied to see who could get the most blood from a sacrificed steer on his toga, thinking that such would prevent death, in came Christianity, proclaiming eternal life, not mortality.

Resurrection and Union with Christ

In verses 20–28, Paul puts two very important things together for us: Christ's resurrection and our union with him. Paul starts out by saying that Christ is "the firstfruits of those who have fallen asleep" (1 Cor. 15:20). This is an agricultural analogy. A good farmer knows what the whole harvest will look like, based on the first sheaf of grain he sees. Here Paul tells us that because of what Christ did in his resurrection the harvest is going to be the best imaginable!

In fact, Christ's resurrection is the beginning of the resurrection of the dead. This is not just reserved for the age to come. Not only does the descent of the Holy Spirit tell us that the age to come has broken into this present evil age, but the resurrection of Christ triumphantly proclaims the same thing. The resurrection of the dead at the end of the age has already begun with its first member, Jesus of Nazareth, our federal and covenant head. The last Adam has been raised in our place.

First Corinthians 15 is not the only place where Paul talks about the two Adams, contrasting the inheritance we have in Adam with the inheritance we have in Christ. He does this also in Romans 5. There are many parallels between what Paul argues in Romans 5 and what he argues here. We have Adam's sin and guilt imputed to us, and his corruption imparted to us. The penalty for this is death. We have Christ's righteousness imputed to us, received by faith alone. Therefore, his eternal life—the state that he now enjoys—is guaranteed to us when he returns. So not only is our spiritual resurrection (which we currently enjoy) a reality, but the coming physical resurrection is as well.

Getting back to Paul's argument in 1 Corinthians 15, we find that he says, "Then comes the end" (v. 24). What is Paul talking about here? Is it the end of the world or the end of time? No, this is not the end of time; this is not the end of the world altogether. Rather, this is "the end of the world, as we know it," to quote the famous song.

Paul continues in verses 24–26:

> Then comes the end, when he delivers the kingdom to God the Father after destroying every rule and every authority and power. For he must reign until he has put all his enemies under his feet. The last enemy to be destroyed is death.

Notice that Paul does not say that everything material will be destroyed—it is very important to note that.

Maybe the best way to understand what Paul means here is to look at the end of his argument. In verse 56, he writes, "The sting of death is sin, and the power of sin is the law." Lying on our deathbeds, it is easy for us to begin to wonder about God and where we are with him. Why? Because there is something in us—in our consciences—that knows that this is not the way it's supposed to be. Death is not natural. We instinctively know that it is not a part of the cycle of life; there is something dreadfully unnatural about death. And Paul says here that death is not the believer's friend to celebrate with, but the believer's enemy to triumph over in the cross.

So death is not natural. Death is God's sentence for sin. Death is the executioner, and it has to execute that sentence according to the dictates of God's holy law. That's why Paul tells us that "the sting of death is sin, and the power of sin is the law." In other words, until our lawbreaking is dealt with, we cannot be raised from the dead. Death is a penalty. Death is a judicial sentence, and until that judicial sentence is removed, God has to consign us to everlasting death. He must do this because of his justice, his holiness, and his righteousness. Not even God can raise you from the dead to eternal life if you are unjust, if you are unrighteous, or if you are unholy. Again, the reason we die in the first place is that God's justice requires it.

No one really dies of natural causes, but of the most horrific and unnatural cause. We die because we have rebelled against our Creator, collectively and individually. So in order for God to raise us bodily from the dead, the judicial sentence has to be removed. We have to be right before God in the sight of the law. Justification, the legal declaration that we are righteous in Christ through faith alone, is the basis for the glorification that we will receive when we are raised immortal in the likeness of Christ.

This is why the general resurrection of the dead didn't happen at Easter. Now is the time when we go out into the whole world and proclaim the forgiveness of sins. We announce the gospel and the good news of the resurrection of Jesus Christ and our participation in his glorious future.

Thus, when Paul says, in verse 28, "When all things are subjected to him, then the Son himself will also be subjected to him who put all things in subjection under him, that God may be all in all," he is fitting it together with the famous thirteenth chapter, in a way. He is saying that the day is coming when we will no longer have faith. We will no longer have hope, because our hope will be fulfilled by the bodily resurrection (cf. Rom. 8:24). We are in a holding pattern, waiting patiently and earnestly for all this to come to pass.

The day is coming when we will only have love. There will be no faith or hope, nothing to wait for, nothing to look forward to in terms of a promise to be fulfilled. There will only be an eternal reality to enjoy forever, which can never be taken away from us.

So here is the order of events: First, Christ's resurrection as the firstfruits. Second, the present intermission, when faith in Christ leads to justification and new life. Third, the return of Christ, who raises the dead. Notice that there is no intervening event like a rapture or anything else. Paul says that what we are looking for now, as we endure suffering and tribulation in this present evil age, is the return of Jesus Christ in the flesh.

Remember the context of all this: Paul is saying that if the resurrection isn't true, then there is no point in being religious, spiritual, or even moral. Paul doesn't say that if the Christian thing doesn't work out, then try Baha'i. Paul's option is this: if this isn't true, become a hedonist. Paul says that if Christianity isn't true, let's not just try something else, but let's eat, drink, and be merry, for tomorrow we die (v. 32).

Resurrection of the Body

Finally, what is the nature of the resurrection? Paul gives his answer in verses 35–49. What he is concerned for us to see is what he has been saying all along. Our problem is not our bodies. Our souls are not somehow the "real" us. We are both body and soul, never meant to be separated. This is why death is so unnatural. But Paul does give us answers here about the relationship between our current bodily existence and the resurrection existence that awaits us.

Paul refers here to three different analogies of bodies. He uses the analogy of seeds first: "what you sow is not the body that is to be, but a bare kernel, perhaps of wheat or of some other grain. But God gives it a body as he has chosen, and to each kind of seed its own body" (1 Cor. 15:37–38). His imagery is that of a kernel of wheat—dry, fragile, and shriveled—which gets tossed to the ground and, behold, next spring a young, vibrant, green shoot pops out of the earth. Who would imagine that what was once dry and shriveled is now this healthy young sprout before us? In its essence, it is the same thing, but the condition is so different that you almost think that they are completely different plants.

Next, Paul says, look at the animals. He notes that their flesh differs from ours. Then Paul turns to the heavens and observes the different degrees of glory there (vv. 39–42). He refers to the sun, the moon, and the stars—created celestial bodies. There is a greater light, and there is a lesser light. This doesn't mean that they are not both light, but there is a different dignity to each one.

How does this relate to our bodies? Our bodies have been sown in dishonor because of the fall, being united to Adam. But, united to Christ, they will be raised in glory and honor. We cannot miss this most important point: not one of these analogies draws any contrast between matter and spirit, as most philosophers, ancient and modern, are wont to do.

How do these analogies relate to our bodies? Paul tells us that we will have the same body, only in a different condition. He says that "what is sown is perishable; what is raised is imperishable" (v. 42). The key here is the continuity between the body that dies and the body that is raised to life. It is not a different body. It is the same body in a different form, in a different condition. He doesn't say that what is sown is physical, and that what is raised is spiritual. Rather, he says that what is sown as perishable is raised imperishable.

But if that is so, then why does Paul contrast the natural body and the spiritual body? We have to realize what Paul is up to here. He is using their native terminology and turning it on its head! For Paul, in the two-age scheme (as opposed to the strict dualism of the Greeks), this present evil age is the age of the flesh—that which is possible is that which we have from the resources of our natural abilities. However, the spirit that Paul is contrasting here refers not to spirit as opposed to matter, but to the Holy Spirit, who brings the age to come. The natural body is what we get from Adam. Adam was a living being, Paul argues here, but not a life-giving being (v. 45). Adam had life, but he didn't give life eternal. He forfeited that life.

The tree of life was held out to Adam as the reward for fulfilling his probation. After that time, he would win for himself and his posterity the right to eat from the tree of life. But he disobeyed and God barred human beings from the tree of life for our own good. If he hadn't, our race would have been confirmed in everlasting death.

But then God opened the way for the second Adam to come, the one who would fulfill all righteousness in everything that Adam failed to do. Jesus Christ would give us the right to eat from the same tree of life that he ate from, so that he in fact became the tree of life. As Adam's descendants, we are living beings, but in Adam we are doomed to die. Yet, assuming our flesh as the last Adam, Jesus also could die. In fact, he did die; he died as the greatest sinner who ever lived—as the sin of his people was imputed to him. He knew exactly what Paul was talking about here, when the apostle said that the sting of death is sin and the strength of sin is the law. Jesus felt the full force of the truth of that statement, more than any human being ever has or ever will.

Christ lost his biological life. He surrendered. He laid down that life that he had from Adam, only to be vindicated and raised, not only as the one who has eternal life, but also as the one who *gives* eternal life to the world. Again, how foreign all this was to the world in which Paul was writing. In the Greek scheme, our true self is raised from the body to heavenly bliss. In Paul's scheme, our whole person is raised from sin and death following in Christ's wake, in the day of our resurrection. The Greek and the average Westerner today were and are looking for an inner light and liberation from this world, from time, and from history. In contrast to this, Christians are looking for the day when what is mortal is "swallowed up by life" (2 Cor. 5:4).

This is what will happen to us on the last day: the resurrection of the body is glorification. It will be a cosmic courtroom event, when all of creation—all of the angels and all of the hosts of heaven—will see us in radiant glory, just like Jesus Christ. That's when everything will be vindicated. Justification will not just be a forensic declaration that we believe in, but on that day we will be, in fullness, everything that the verdict of justification declares. In other words, the Holy Spirit doesn't come to make the old Adam a little better; the Spirit comes to kill us, so that we fall to the ground like that fragile, shriveled kernel of wheat, only to raise us under Christ's auspices.

Not in Vain

Paul finishes by saying, "Here are the practical benefits to what I am saying."

When the perishable puts on the imperishable, and the mortal puts on immortality, then shall come to pass the saying that is written: "Death is swallowed up in victory." "O death, where is your victory? O death, where is your sting?" The sting of death is sin, and the power of sin is the law. But thanks be to God, who gives us the victory through our Lord Jesus Christ. Therefore, my beloved brothers, be steadfast, immovable, always abounding in the work of the Lord, knowing that in the Lord your labor is not in vain. (1 Cor. 15:54-58)

Look at how this frees us to live for Christ and to love our neighbors! Someone asked Martin Luther what he would do if he knew Christ was coming back tomorrow. Luther said, "I would plant a tree." Nothing fancy—just loving and serving our neighbor as we wait for Christ to come.

Perhaps someone would want to ask Luther further, "Why would you beautify the world, if it's all going to burn up?" This is the "Late, Great Planet Earth" school of thought. Is this the mentality we should have? Not if we're looking for the resurrection of the body and the life everlasting. Paul says our hope is not in vain, and neither are our labors in this age.

Even now, the age to come is breaking in upon us, Paul says. The future hope is not something we are passively waiting for; it is something that actively motivates and renews us in this life. This will happen as we faithfully take up our posts in this world—in our families, in our homes, and in our neighborhoods. Why? Because Christ has died, Christ has risen, and Christ will come again.

5

The Eternal Glory

J. LIGON DUNCAN III

Then I saw a new heaven and a new earth, for the first heaven and the first earth had passed away, and the sea was no more. (Revelation 21:1)

ONE OF THE FASCINATING things about biblical eschatology—the study of the end times—is how consistently the Bible connects these grand themes to daily life. In fact, it regularly teaches that eschatology is directly connected to ethics, to how we are to live the Christian life right now. It is important for us to remember this even when we consider something like the coming eternal glory. Indeed, we must not forget that God intends for us to understand these things that he has written in his word—things that " 'no eye has seen, nor ear heard, nor the heart of man imagined, what God has prepared for those who love him'—these things God has revealed to us through the Spirit" (1 Cor. 2:9–10). God intends for us, then, to understand and meditate on these things.

Being Heavenly Minded

The last two chapters of the Bible, Revelation 21 and 22, form one of the great passages that God gives to us to meditate on the eternal glory. Jonathan Edwards made it a practice to meditate on the new heavens and the new earth—the eternal glory—every day. But today, very often we hear people say that a person is "so heavenly minded that he is no earthly good." The biblical way of thinking is the direct opposite of this. The Bible insists that you cannot be earthly good unless you are heavenly minded. Heavenly mindedness actually promotes our discipleship here on earth, and it gives us the assurance that we do not labor in vain.

This reminds me of a story, which involves a Presbyterian minister. Once, when he was walking through the streets of a city, he came upon a shoeshine stand. There was a little boy industriously shining shoes, and the Presbyterian minister came upon him. He noticed that the boy had a book open. He looked closer and saw that it was a Bible. As he looked even closer, the little boy seemed to be reading from the end of the Bible. So the minister said, "What you are reading there, son?" The little boy replied, "I am reading the Bible." "What book of the Bible are you reading?" the minister inquired. The little boy answered, "Why, I am reading the book of Revelation." The minister sort of snorted and said, "Well, do you understand what you are reading?" The little boy smiled and replied, "Yes, sir, I do." The minister (somewhat condescendingly) said, "Well, why don't you explain the book of Revelation to me?" The little boy grinned and said, "It's simple: we win." Now, that is exactly the point of the book of Revelation!

It is vital for us as we live the Christian life to understand this simple point that the little boy made about the book of Revelation. So very often in this life, we are called to lose, in a sense, if we are Christians. Sometimes we are called to win in the sense of achieving some of our dreams. These may be very good dreams, fine dreams—even biblical dreams. But when we achieve these things, we are tempted to think that they were the best things, the greatest treasures. But there are yet greater treasures to come, and that's why we must meditate on the eternal glory.

In the final three chapters of Revelation, John unfolds for us the most beautiful theme of the book. In fact, in the last three chapters, he actually revisits the first three chapters of the Bible and he tells us how the story ends. Think of it: In Genesis 1, we have the record of God creating the heavens and the earth. In Revelation 21, we have the unfolding of the new heavens and earth. In Genesis 1, we have the creation of the great luminaries, the sun and the moon, which control our lives, structure its rhythm, and order life on this world. In Revelation 21, we are presented with a world in which the sun and the moon are no longer necessary, for God and the Lamb will be the light of their people.

In Genesis 3, we witness paradise lost; in Revelation 22, paradise is restored. In Genesis 3, we encounter a crafty devil; in Revelation 20, we encounter a condemned devil. In Genesis 3, fellowship with God is broken; in Revelation 21, eternal communion with God is consummated. In Genesis 3, access to the tree of life is denied; in Revelation 22, the right of access to the tree of life, whose leaves are for the healing of the nations, is restored.

In the final chapters of the Bible, John is deliberately telling us the end of the story that began at the beginning of the Bible. There are five things in particular that I want to look at in this great passage. We can organize these five things by five words. They are: God, Jesus, the church, worship, and communion.

John, in this vision that he received in the Spirit on the Lord's Day (1:10), is given a glimpse of what is to come. He is permitted to write down some of this vision in order to tell us what is to come, so that we might take heart to live the Christian life now. It is almost as if John is on a ladder, looking into the future, looking into a reality that is not yet experienced by any of God's people. Even those who have gone on to glory have not experienced this final eternal glory, which will be unveiled after the reign of Jesus Christ is commenced at his second coming. No one will enjoy these realities until all of God's people enjoy them simultaneously. We will all see these things together at the same time.

A God-Produced Heaven

John has been given a picture of what is to come. And, as I said, it is almost as if John is on a ladder, shouting back to us, "This is what I see!" The first thing he says, as he turns back to us, is this: "God is here!" Well, that doesn't surprise us at all. But I want you to look especially at what he says in Revelation 21:2: "And I saw the holy city, new Jerusalem, coming down out of heaven from God, prepared as a bride adorned for her husband." What John is telling us here is that the whole reality that he sees is produced by God. It is God who has accomplished this great reality of the new heavens and the new earth. This is further signified by the new Jerusalem coming down from heaven. It is not built up from earth; it comes down from God. It is prepared by God.

Now, this is vitally important for us as we seek to understand our role in this world. So often *we* want to build God's kingdom. But the Bible never uses that language of us in relation to God's kingdom. The New Testament insists that there is only one who builds the kingdom—and it's not you or me. It is God. We may pray for the kingdom, we may preach for the kingdom, and we may live for the kingdom, but it's God who builds and brings the kingdom. Surely that lesson is on John's mind in this passage—that God is the one who produces the reality of the new heavens and earth. He is the one who builds the new Jerusalem and sends it down. It is something that has been produced and created by God. Why do I belabor this point? Because oftentimes we are called to serve the Lord faithfully in this life, never seeing the ends that we desire achieved.

This is illustrated by one of the most well-known creeds in Christendom. Many of us have benefited from the work of a group of English, Scottish, Welsh, and Irish Puritans from the middle of the seventeenth century called the Westminster Confession of Faith. Now, it's perfectly fine if you have never read this document; it basically describes what the Bible teaches concerning just about any theological topic you can imagine. This was written by men who had a great desire to see all the churches in England, Scotland, Wales, and Ireland share the same theology and worship, as well as the same view of the doctrines of the Christian life and the church. But it never happened. Their vision never came to pass. These men spent seven years of hard labor producing this confession and other documents that they hoped would bring about a reformation in the churches of these countries. And it never happened.

However, today there are nine million East Africans who believe that the Westminster Confession of Faith is the most faithful description of what the Bible teaches. Now, those men of the Westminster Assembly in the 1640s and 1650s, when they never saw their goal achieved, could have been very discouraged. They didn't know how the Lord was going to use their lives and labors. But it didn't matter then, and it doesn't matter now. God has called us to faithfulness, and he will build his kingdom in his own way.

This kind of thing didn't just happen in the seventeenth century. Think of the greatest prophet of the Old Testament, Moses, who spent forty years leading grumbling, recalcitrant Hebrews through the wilderness. He finally gets in view of the Promised Land and says, "I just can't wait to go into the Promised Land!" But the Lord says to him, "You're not going into the land, Moses" (see Num. 20:12). Can you imagine how Moses must have felt? He may have been tempted to think, "I have spent forty years with these people, and I don't even get to go into the Promised Land!" But did he do that? No. When Moses died and opened his eyes, he was already seeing a greater thing than the children of Israel would see when they went into Canaan. And he will see yet greater things in the eternal age to come!

So, God often calls us to labor faithfully here, even when we do not see the end of our labors realized. This is why here, at the end of the book of Revelation, he points us to a reality that he himself will bring about. No matter how fruitful or how frustrating our labor may be here, God will not waste the labors of his people. The reality that he will give to us will far outstrip anything that we can imagine, anything that we have accomplished, or any frustration that we have experienced in this life. Again, this is so vitally important for us to remember. So the first thing John tells us—our first word—is that the new heavens and the new earth are God-produced and God-created.

A Jesus-Focused Heaven

The second thing we hear about the new heavens and the new earth from John is that they are Jesus-focused. First, John shouted back to us, "God is here!" Now John shouts back, "They are all about Jesus up here!" They are singing praises to Jesus, and they are worshiping him. Jesus is the center of everything. John tells us that this is the case on a number of levels.

Notice the inclusion of God and the Lamb in verse 22: "And I saw no temple in the city, for its temple is the Lord God the Almighty and the Lamb." This theme occurs again in 22:1–3:

> Then the angel showed me the river of the water of life, bright as crystal, flowing from the throne of God and of the Lamb through the middle of the street of the city; also, on either side of the river, the tree of life with its twelve kinds of fruit, yielding its fruit each month. The leaves of the tree were for the healing of the nations. No longer will there be anything accursed, but the throne of God and of the Lamb will be in it, and his servants will worship him.

So Jesus is the focus of the worship of the saints in heaven. He is worshiped as the divine Son of God on the throne in heaven. This is so critical in our day, because all around us—even in churches—the uniqueness of Jesus Christ and the necessity of Jesus Christ for salvation are both being called into question. This is happening in places where, if we had been told fifty years ago that these things would be questioned, it would have elicited laughter on our part. So we need to listen to John again. He tells us that in glory people are worshiping Jesus.

Now what does John's vision say to people who claim that there is a way to God other than through faith in the Lord Jesus Christ? Let us answer with another question: where are those different "ways" and "saviors" when John watches the worship of heaven? John doesn't record any other ways or saviors being worshiped, because there are none. Jesus is the only way—that is why he is being worshiped.

Jesus is being worshiped because he is the true and only Savior, whose death alone is sufficient to cover the sins of his people. But there are many people who are going to get to the great day of judgment and say, "You know, I was a good person, I tried to live a godly life. I tried to be kind to my neighbors. I tried to follow the Golden Rule." What they don't realize is that, when they think things like this now and plead with God on that day then, they are saying to God that it wasn't necessary for Jesus to die on the cross. They are basically saying to God, "Thank you for sending your Son to die—that might have been necessary for some wretches out there, but it wasn't necessary for me. I was a good enough person on my own!"

Now, can you imagine what God the Father is going to say in response? He may say something like, "Are you saying that it was not necessary for me to give my Son? Are you saying that it was not necessary for me to hear his cries of dereliction and abandonment because you were good enough?" We can be sure that the Father will not listen to such nonsense from us. He would not have given his Son, his only Son, whom he loves, had there been some other way for us to enter into fellowship with him. The sacrifice of Christ is such an expensive gift that we will sing for eternity about it. So this is what John is picturing for us: people who are focused on Jesus. Why are they focused on Jesus? Because he is the one who has brought them to God.

Recently I had the pleasure of reading Jonathan Aitken's biography of John Newton, *From Disgrace to Amazing Grace*.[1] I was reading the chapter that covers the final months of Newton's life when he was losing his faculties. Newton was at the point where he could not preach because he could not keep his mind on any particular subject. Very often he would get up in the pulpit and have to ask the congregation what he was supposed to be preaching! He had friends for several months saying, "Brother John, you are past your time to preach; you need to commit yourself to praying for and loving and serving God's people instead."

In particular, Newton forgot the entire liturgy of his final wedding service. He had to ask the congregation several times what he was supposed to do at a certain point. They would respond and tell him what to do. How sad it was to see this great man losing his mind. But during his final days, one of his dearest friends came to him. Newton simply said to this man, "I have almost lost everything, but this I remember: I am a great sinner and Jesus is a great Savior." In heaven those are going to be our watchwords! We are great sinners and Jesus is a great Savior.

There is a third thing that John tells us he sees. We may be saying, "Okay, we are not surprised to see God there. We are not surprised to see Jesus there. But, tell us, John, what do you see there? What is it like?" And John answers with descriptions that are predominantly negative. Look at Revelation 21:1: "Then I saw a new heaven and a new earth, for the first heaven and the first earth had passed away, and the sea was no more." Now, this may disturb some people, because we like the sea. We like to

1. Jonathan Aitken, *John Newton: From Disgrace to Amazing Grace* (Wheaton, IL: Crossway, 2007).

go down to the beach and watch the waves crashing in. But to the Hebrew people the sea was something dangerous. After all, the Israelites were not known as a great seafaring nation. One never sees a book entitled *Great Heroes of the Hebrew Navy*! No, they were afraid of the sea. The sea was filled with terrors and storms. So I think John is just reminding us in a picturesque way that there will be no danger in the new heavens and the new earth. Danger is done away with; John tells us this in a beautiful, polite way.

Now, if we look down at verse 4, we see another negative description: "He will wipe away every tear from their eyes, and death shall be no more, neither shall there be mourning nor crying nor pain anymore, for the former things have passed away." When what John is seeing here comes to pass, never again will a pastor look at a woman with her lifeless, breathless infant in her arms. Never again will there be funerals for our loved ones. John calls back to us, in a triumphant tone, "There is no danger here! There is no death here! There is no mourning here! There is no crying here! There is no pain here!" He is telling us all the things that he does not see there—and how precious are these descriptions!

One of my finest students in twenty years of teaching seminary has a wife who has been diagnosed with a chronic pain disorder. She cannot breathe without pain. She cannot swallow without pain. She cannot open a drawer without pain. She is unable to pick up her children. On top of this, she is caring for a child with cystic fibrosis. Another one of my dear friends in Britain, a minister in the Free Church, has a wife who is vexed with so much chronic nerve pain that she cannot sleep at night. She has not slept in twenty years. She catnaps sitting upright in a chair, and she sings hymns to herself. She blesses us by writing children's books. She does this in the middle of the night when she can't sleep on account of the pain. She has written a wonderful book about her difficulties entitled *Pain, My Companion*.[2] But in the new heavens and the new earth, for my student's wife and my friend's wife, pain will be no more.

A Church-Filled Heaven

But we still want to say to John, "Okay, John, you've told us what is not there, but we still want to know what *is* there!" Here is what John tells us in Revelation 21:2: "And I saw the holy city, new Jerusalem, coming down out of heaven from God, prepared as a bride adorned for her husband." He says the same thing in a slightly different way in verse 9: "Then came one of the seven angels who had the seven bowls full of the seven last plagues and spoke to me, saying, 'Come, I will show you the Bride, the wife of the Lamb.'" So John is calling back to us, "The church is here! The bride of Christ—men and women and boys and girls from every tribe, tongue, people, and nation—is here!" What a glorious depiction this is of the consummation of God's great plan to redeem a people for himself.

This is why it is so good for us to gather as brothers and sisters in Christ under his Word, from different churches and congregations, to celebrate that day, so beautifully described by the hymn writer: "From earth's wide bounds, from ocean's farthest coast, through gates of pearl streams in the countless host, singing to Father, Son, and Holy Ghost!"[3] We gather together on the Lord's Day to anticipate that day when all of God's children are brought in together.

2. Irene Howat, *Pain, My Companion* (Ross-shire, UK: Christian Focus, 1969).
3. William Walsham How, "For All the Saints" (1864, 1875).

The church, then, will be the only monument of God's glory that stands for all eternity. This world is only a workshop, set up by God to stand for a little while until his work is done. Then he will close the workshop and reveal his masterpiece: the church. He looks for no other glory but what he sees in his Son's bride, the church. According to John, this is God's metropolis, his temple, and his house.

Now the church may not look like much to you today. She may not look like much to you at all. You may have experienced the church at her failing, betraying, and disappointing worst. But God is not done with his people yet. And when he unveils her at the last day, she is going to positively take your breath away. Indeed, over the centuries he has been adorning a bride that he will present to his Son. John sees her in her perfection here at the end of Revelation, and it is glorious.

Again, John Newton illustrates this well. He produced a volume of letters that he wrote to his wife, which are very loving even by today's standards, but especially for the late 1700s. He was very expressive about his love for his wife. In fact, one of his friends who reviewed the book condemned it, believe it or not. His friend said that when Christian ladies read Newton's book, it would cause great problems for husbands because Newton was so passionate in his expressions of love for his wife. His friend feared that all wives were going to expect the same kind of passion from their husbands, and, well, that was just not good!

But the interesting thing about Newton's letters to his wife is this: his dearest friends never saw what Newton saw in his wife. To be quite frank, they didn't think she had much in the way of looks or brains. Newton seemed to understand this as well. On one occasion, after his wife's death, Newton wrote to William Wilberforce, his good friend. Newton compared his late wife to a pineapple (not a recommended analogy, husbands). He basically said that while his wife may have been prickly and unattractive on the outside, like a good pineapple she had to be experienced to know how glorious she truly was on the inside. He understood his friends' concerns, but his wife was glorious to him.

So it is with Christ and his church. She is glorious to him. You may not see what's glorious about the church to God, but he is going to show you. This is why it is so important for us to love the church now—with all her imperfections, all her weaknesses, all her failures, and all her stumblings. One day, God is going to unveil her, and she is going to take your breath away.

There is, in the midst of this captivating scene that John unfolds for us, something dark that we dare not overlook. Look at what he says in verse 27: "But nothing unclean will ever enter it, nor anyone who does what is detestable or false, but only those who are written in the Lamb's book of life."

John is reminding us here of something else that he doesn't see in the new heavens and new earth. He does not see those who have lived in wickedness. He does not see those who did not trust in the Lamb. They are not there. He is reminding us of the reality of hell, even in the final chapter of the Bible, where he is painting a picture of glory.

A number of years ago, a friend of mine in Scotland, who has twice been named the Scottish Journalist of the Year, wrote an article on hell for the largest daily newspaper in Scotland, the *Glasgow Herald*. He wrote an article on hell—can you imagine an article on hell appearing in the op-ed section of the *New York Times*? The editorial was entitled "Between a Hard Place and Satan's Spandau." You will recall that Spandau was the infamous Nazi prison. I want to share with you what John Macleod said about hell in his article. It was the most widely read and responded to article in the history of the *Glasgow Herald*. Let me quote Macleod at length:

Hell flows logically from the teaching of scripture. The terrible end that awaits the ungodly is stressed from Genesis to Revelation; as much part of the New Testament as the Old. Indeed, Jesus in the Gospels refers more often to Hell than anyone else in the Bible. He believes in it in sober earnest; after all He created it. For Hell is not the kingdom of Satan. Hell will be Satan's Spandau. . . .

I have never doubted the reality of such a place; a Hades of deep and lasting darkness. But I have never thought of it in popular terms, as a rather nasty boiler room run by wee men in red tights. Hell is ultimately a negative, a place of nothing but anguish: it is a place without God, and without anything of God, without light, without warmth, without friendship and without peace. No racks, no pincers, no claws: only the fires of an awakened conscience, the burning thirst of frustrated ego. . . .

This I believe. And I believe too that there is only one escape, by flight to Christ and faith in His finished work, living in His service but never looking to such toils for my salvation. But there is this final paradox: to believe in this latter end of all things, and to live and walk in a world that must one day melt in fervent heat—to walk among the living dead, with my bright smile and polite talk, and never to challenge, and never warn.[4]

The apostle John is reminding us of the reality of this awful place even as he is encouraging us with a picture of eternal glory. He is reminding us of the importance of being gospel men and women, of being those who are living out the truth. He is calling us to be those who are sharing the gospel with others, that they might join in the blessing of eternal glory.

4. John Macleod, "Between a Hard Place and Satan's Spandau (Or, Why I Believe in Hell)," *The Glasgow Herald*, April 28, 1992.

A Worship-Preoccupied Heaven

But there is a fourth thing that we see here in this great passage: worship. John shows us a God-produced new heavens and new earth. He shows us a Jesus-focused heaven. He shows us a church-filled heaven. He then shows us a worship-preoccupied heaven. Notice that the worship of God and of the Lamb is the framework for the whole scene. Revelation 22:3 makes this explicit: "But the throne of God and of the Lamb will be in it, and his servants will worship him." So, heaven is a place of worship.

What is worship? Worship is essentially giving to the Lord the glory due his name. But it's very important for us to understand that Christians are not the only people that worship. Everybody worships something. We worship what we value most. Worship says, "This person, this thing, this activity, this status, and this blessing are what I value most." And in heaven, the triune God and fellowship and communion with him are the things valued most.

You can find out what people worship by following the trail of their time, money, interests, desires, and ambitions. Follow these and at the end of the trail you will find a throne, and on that throne you will find something or someone. This someone or something on the throne is what that person worships. It might be sex. It might be money. It might be power. Or it might be recognition or acceptance. To be sure, we don't often walk around saying, "I worship sex" or "I worship my body" or "I worship food" or "I worship her." But the trail of our time and our interests never lies.

The world is, therefore, not divided between people who worship and people who don't. It is divided between people who worship God and people who worship everything else. And in heaven, worship is focused on God. Here, perhaps more than anywhere else, we see the difference between Christians and those who worship everything else.

The unbeliever chooses heaven only because he is scared of hell. But the believer chooses heaven over earth, to paraphrase the great Puritan, Richard Baxter. Now why did Baxter say that? He said it because nobody wants to go to hell. But—and here is where believers can begin to get uncomfortable—we show what we really want by what we worship. If we show that we want this earth more than we want God, then we are worshiping our wills. We are worshiping something or someone other than God.

But if we say, "No, I want God. I want heaven more even than I want this earth," then we show that we worship God. So, at the end of our lives, we really find out what people want and what people worship. Heaven will be a place in which people worship God because they have chosen to worship him here.

A Communion-Blessed Heaven

There is one last thing we see here. John tells us of a communion-blessed place. Notice the phrase that's repeated several times in this great passage. The idea of God being our God, and of us enjoying communion with him as his children, is repeated in this passage (see Rev. 21:3, 7). This is the ultimate end of God's covenant purposes: our union and communion with him. So, John shouts back to us, "I see communion here!"

Look at the amazing language of 22:4: "They will see his face, and his name will be on their foreheads." John is speaking of communion, of fellowship with the living God. It's what we were created for, but lost. Our sin made God cry, "Go away from here!" The way to communion and fellowship with him was barred. But the Lord Jesus Christ has drawn near to us and said, "Come to me, all who labor and are heavy laden, and I will give you rest" (Matt. 11:28). The ultimate consummation of that invitation is found right here, in glory, when we do, in fact, see God face-to-face. It will be consummated when we, at last, dwell with him and commune with him and fellowship with him.

It's really what the end of the Twenty-third Psalm is saying as well. The language of dwelling "in the house of the LORD forever" is the language of intimate communion. I love the way that Isaac Watts paraphrases the end of this psalm: "There would I find a settled rest, while others go and come; no more a stranger, nor a guest, but like a child at home."

In my days of graduate school in St. Louis, I used to drive home to see my family. Toward the end of those drives, I remember thinking to myself, "If I can just get home, everything will be all right." When I drove across Interstate 40 to Interstate 26 and then on to Highway 25, I felt better by the time I got to the South Carolina border. However, when I finally stepped across that threshold on 640 McDaniel Avenue, I knew I was safe because I was home, where I was loved.

This same feeling is what every believer will experience on that great day. We will look around and say, "Finally! I am home with my Father, who loved me and gave his Son for me." Every believer will be there with the saints, angels, archangels, and elders, with men and women and boys and girls from every tribe and tongue and people and nation, who are now my brothers and sisters in Christ. We will say, "I'm home, at last!"

In this world, we have no lasting city, but in the new heavens and earth we do. There is a city there with foundations, whose architect and builder is God, to borrow the language of Hebrews. He is our Father, and he will say, "Child, welcome home." That's what John tells us he sees. But even John won't see the fullness of that glory until the eyes of every one of us who trusts in Jesus Christ see it together. So, my friend, see to it that you trust in Christ now and that you do not fail to meditate on the eternal glory to come.

6

Partakers of the Age to Come

D. A. CARSON

[Christ is seated] far above all rule and authority and power and dominion, and above every name that is named, not only in this age but also in the one to come. (Ephesians 1:21)

THIS IS A BOOK ABOUT eschatology. Our English word comes from the Greek word *eschatos*, which simply means "last." Eschatology, then, is what the Bible says about last things. But Christians know that the subject is a little more complicated than that! As we study eschatology, I would like for us to begin our study in Ephesians 1:15–23, and I want to make some preliminary observations regarding eschatology in general before going in depth into this passage. Read what God says:

> For this reason, because I have heard of your faith in the Lord Jesus and your love toward all the saints, I do not cease to give thanks for you, remembering you in my prayers, that the God of our Lord Jesus Christ, the Father of glory, may give you a spirit of wisdom and of revelation in the knowledge of him, having the eyes of your hearts enlightened, that you may know what is the hope to which he has called you, what are the riches of his glorious inheritance in the saints, and what is the immeasurable greatness of his power toward us who believe, according to the working of his great might that he worked in Christ when he raised him from the dead and seated him at his right hand in the heavenly places, far above all rule and authority and power and dominion, and above every name that is named, not only in this age but also in the one to come. And he put all things under his feet and gave him as head over all things to the church, which is his body, the fullness of him who fills all in all.

By way of preliminary observation, notice that the New Testament says that it is already the last hour. We are already in the last days, according to the Bible. Moreover, the New Testament shows how Christians are squeezed between the "already" of what has arrived and the "not yet" of what is still to come. Let me give you some examples: we already have the forgiveness of our sins, but we do not yet have the consummation which Christ's death and resurrection have secured. We already grow in sanctification, but we have not yet been glorified. We are squeezed between the already and the not yet; already it is the last hour of this age which is decaying and will pass away. But it has not yet passed away, and the new heavens and the new earth have not yet dawned.

Over- and Under-Realized Eschatologies

It is clear, then, that we live in this tension of the already and the not yet. Furthermore, the New Testament shows how Christians can go sadly astray by getting this balance wrong. This leads to what is sometimes called an "over-realized eschatology." That is, you think that you have more of the blessings from the future now than you actually do. Or one can suffer from having an "under-realized eschatology." That is, you really don't appreciate what you have in your possession. The New Testament witnesses to both sorts of errors.

For example, Paul writes to the Corinthians, in 1 Corinthians 4:8–11, somewhat sarcastically:

> Already you have all you want! Already you have become rich! Without us you have become kings! And would that you did reign, so that we might share the rule with you! For I think that God has exhibited us apostles as last of all, like men sentenced to death, because we have become a spectacle to the world, to angels, and to men. We are fools for Christ's sake, but you are wise in Christ. We are weak, but you are strong. You are held in honor, but we in disrepute. To the present hour we hunger and thirst, we are poorly dressed and buffeted and homeless.

Do you see that? The Corinthians sound not a little like some contemporary health, wealth, and prosperity gospel people, do they not? Isn't the reasoning today the same as the Corinthian reasoning back then? "After all," some surely said, "you are the child of the king; doesn't your dad want you to have everything?" Well, yes, we could say that—but he also wants you to be disciplined. He also wants you to learn something of suffering like his Son, before everything is opened up in the new heavens and the new earth.

But did you see here that over-realized eschatology leads to a kind of triumphalism that seems to think that everything that you are going to get in the future you get right now? Healing, transformed personalities that approach sinless perfection, perfect love, perfect marriages, perfect wealth, perfect satisfaction, perfect contentment—it's all yours right now! Name it; claim it! After all, Christ has secured it.

By way of reply, we could say, well, yes, all the blessings that we will ever enjoy, Christ has secured. But we are squeezed between the already and the not yet. And if you have an over-realized eschatology, you will imagine that you have some things that are actually reserved for the final healing in the final transformation and the final glorification of God's people on the last day.

On the other hand, if you have an under-realized eschatology, you will fail to appreciate what you actually have in Christ Jesus now. You not only have the forgiveness of sins and the joy of being once and for all declared just before God because of what Christ has done, but also have ongoing cleansing from sin! What a blessed relief that is for God's people day by day. He has poured his Spirit out upon us, so that we begin to love what we didn't love and hate what we didn't hate. Our personalities are changed, our goals are changed, our values are changed, and our direction is changed. All of this is because the gospel is the power of God for salvation to those who believe (Rom. 1:16). It is not merely some declaration of a status and that's all. It is also *power*.

This power works itself out in transformed relationships in the community of the saints. So many blessings come to us from God! We must appreciate them, live in the light of them, and grow in them in anticipation of the final transformation that still lies ahead. So part of Christian maturity turns on grasping exactly what it means to be partakers of the age to come. It turns, in part, on getting this balance right.

Now, we shall approach Paul's thought in three steps. I warn you, we are going to go right through Ephesians! Here are our three headings: First, how people become partakers of the age to come. Second, how Paul prayed for the partakers of the age to come. Third, and finally, how God provides for the partakers of the age to come.

Partakers of the Age to Come

Let us look, then, first of all, at how people become partakers of the age to come. That's the burden of the earlier verses in the passage from Ephesians that I quoted above. To do this, we need to go back to the verses immediately prior, verses 3–14. Our section begins with these words in verse 15: "For this reason, because I have heard of your faith in the Lord Jesus and your love toward all the saints." To find out what "this reason" is, we have to read the preceding lines. Those lines turn out to be a spectacular Trinitarian grounding of our salvation. It is helpful, if you read through verses 3–14, to look for the play of several themes.

The first theme is the fulfillment of times; that is, something has taken place in Christ that has fulfilled an antecedent prophecy. We are now at a turning point in history, in other words. Second, there is the theme of the centrality of the cross. Third, Paul gives us the theme of the linking together of Jew and Gentile—in principle, of all races in a new humanity. Fourth, there is a tension between what we already have in Christ and what is still to come. Let me run through some of this quickly.

Paul begins by pointing us, first, to the Father of our Lord Jesus Christ,

> who has blessed us in Christ with every spiritual blessing in the
> heavenly places, even as he chose us in him before the foundation

of the world, that we should be holy and blameless before him. In love he predestined us for adoption through Jesus Christ, according to the purpose of his will, to the praise of his glorious grace, with which he has blessed us in the Beloved. (vv. 3–6)

Here Paul explains the work of the Father in his sovereign plan of predestination, worked out in the gift of his Son to capture us and make us his.

Paul continues in verse 7: "In him we have redemption through his blood, the forgiveness of our trespasses, according to the riches of his grace." Now we have the work of Christ on the cross. Our redemption turns on what Jesus has done—dying on our behalf, bearing our sins in his own body on the tree. We have been redeemed because of what Jesus has done, and as a result we enjoy the forgiveness of sins in accordance with the riches of God's grace,

which he lavished upon us, in all wisdom and insight making known to us the mystery of his will, according to his purpose, which he set forth in Christ as a plan for the fullness of time. (vv. 8–10)

The apostle is telling us that this was God's plan all along, though it was hidden in some ways, but now is unpacked, revealed, and disclosed in Christ Jesus, at this turning point of the ages. Christ has come, and we see how his plans laid out in eternity past, before the creation of the world, have come to pass in one short weekend in Jerusalem.

Rising from the dead, ascending to the right hand of the Majesty on high, this Son pours out his Spirit, for we go on to read this:

In him we have obtained an inheritance, having been predestined according to the purpose of him who works all things according to the counsel of his will, so that we who were the first to hope in Christ might be to the praise of his glory. In him you also, when you heard the word of truth, the gospel of your salvation, and believed in him, were sealed with the promised Holy Spirit. (vv. 11–13)

Thus, the entire triune God is working out our salvation. This is how people become partakers of the age to come. Did you notice that? When you believed, you were marked in him with a seal. I do not know about you, but this seems alien to me! But lift your heart heavenward and cry to God, "Lord, I believe; help my unbelief!" This is God's means of bringing people into the spectacular tension between the ages, by which we become partakers of the age to come.

How Paul Prays

In the second place, let us examine how Paul prays for the partakers of the age to come. We will now focus on what I quoted at the beginning of this chapter, verses 15–23. Let me draw your attention to two details in the text before we follow its flow.

Sometimes people speak of the "Pauline triad," by which they mean faith, hope, and love. It is stunning how often these three show up at the same place in Paul's writings. Occasionally just two of these three are mentioned, but very often all three are given together. The passage I suspect we all know that displays these three together is the last verse of the so-called "Love Chapter," concluding in 1 Corinthians 13:13: "So now faith, hope, and love abide, these three; but the greatest of these is love." Returning to Ephesians 1, here is what we find in verse 15: "For this reason, because I have heard of your faith in the Lord Jesus and your love toward all the saints." So there are two members of Paul's triad. The third is found in verse 18, where Paul prays that "having the eyes of your hearts enlightened . . . you may know what is the hope to which he has called you, what are the riches of his glorious inheritance in the saints."

How these three play out in different passages varies hugely. For example, in Colossians 1:5, hope becomes the grounding of the other two. In that passage, we find the apostle saying that the hope and anticipation of the future is what draws out our faith and gives us motive and incentive to love one another in Christ even now.

In Ephesians, however, Paul speaks of what he has already heard about the Ephesians, namely, their faith in Christ and their love for one another. Now he prays that their eyes might be opened up and enabled to see, so that they may know the hope to which God had called them—and us. The idea, here, is that we cannot be mature Christians unless we are future oriented. By future oriented, I don't mean merely the next ten minutes or even the next ten years. I mean eternity oriented.

I recall, a number of years ago, leading the Bible study at the Bell Labs in Chicago. The Christian I knew there observed that at the lunch break various clubs were formed, so he thought, "If they can start clubs, I can start one too." So he organized a Bible club, and it was just for the scientists in his unit, around thirty-seven of them. The format was simple enough: for eight weeks, I would teach something from the Bible for about twenty minutes, while they ate their lunches. After that, they would ask questions for thirty minutes or so.

The man who got this whole thing started was the only Christian in this group, besides me. There were also a failed Buddhist, a failed Hindu, a failed Catholic, a failed Lutheran, and the rest were unbelievers. So we had a fairly biblically illiterate group, and I was trying to unpack the Bible for them.

On about week five or so, I was dealing with Matthew 6:19–21:

> Do not lay up for yourselves treasures on earth, where moth and rust destroy and where thieves break in and steal, but lay up for yourselves treasures in heaven, where neither moth nor rust destroys and where thieves do not break in and steal. For where your treasure is, there your heart will be also.

I noted that this passage does not tell us to guard our heart; it tells us to choose our treasure. I noted further that the reason for this was that what you treasure most is where your heart will go.

One of the group members, a Hindu chap, said, "Do I understand you right?" I asked him, "What do you think I have said?" "Well," he began, "this is a pretty good research establishment. There are several Nobel laureates amongst us, we have a good budget, excellent projects, and most of us are really glad to be here. We have worked hard to get where we are, and we have our lives pretty well mapped out. Who knows, but maybe two or three more of us will get Nobel prizes in the next few years. We will work hard and advance, and at the age of sixty-five we will retire. We'll continue on as consultants and hire ourselves out in this or that way, write a couple of books that we were unable to write while working, and then produce some more technical papers. We will slow down a wee bit and then play with our grandchildren, and after that it gets a bit fuzzy. But you are saying that Jesus says we shouldn't plan for the next thirty years. We should plan for the next fifty billion or so. Is that right?" I replied, "That sounds exactly right to me. That is what Jesus is talking about."

Did you see that? Remember that Paul has prayed that "having the eyes of your hearts enlightened . . . you may know what is the hope to which he has called you, what are the riches of his glorious inheritance in the saints" (Eph. 1:18). He then unpacks what these riches are in the next verses: "the immeasurable greatness of his power toward us who believe, according to the working of his great might that he worked in Christ when he raised him from the dead and seated him at his right hand in the heavenly places" (vv. 19–20). Paul wants them to know that the incomparably great power for us who believe is the same power that God exerted when he raised Christ from the dead.

We quote often enough the statement that the gospel is the power of God for salvation. But what kind of power? Well, the same miraculous power that raised Jesus from the dead. What kind of divine power was that? Jesus was not just brought back to ordinary life, like Lazarus was, but transformed into resurrection existence with capacities that are beyond anything we know and experience here. Oh yes, Jesus could be touched, he could eat food, he could be recognized, and the wounds were still there, but now he was so utterly transformed that he belonged to both time and eternity. He appeared and disappeared at will. We don't understand this resurrection body very well, but I do know that the power that transformed Christ and brought him back is the power already at work in us, which will then transform us with resurrection bodies on the last day. That's what Paul prays for.

Notice again the Trinitarian references that run right through this text. "I do not cease to give thanks for you, remembering you in my prayers, that the God of our Lord Jesus Christ, the Father of glory, may give you a spirit of wisdom and of revelation in the knowledge of him" (vv. 16–17). All of this focuses on Christ. This is how Paul prays for the partakers of the age to come. What we need to understand is the practical outworking of what it means to be partakers of the age to come.

If you have been a Christian in a Bible-teaching church for a long time, you will know that Christians are caught between the already and not yet. Already we have the Holy Spirit as the guarantee of the promised inheritance. But how does this truth work itself out in our lives? What does it look like? In fact, much of the rest of Ephesians is devoted to answering questions like that.

How God Provides

So, third and finally, let us examine how God provides for the partakers of the age to come. We will do this by briefly noting six things. Of necessity, I will need to spend more time on the first three—not because the last three are unimportant; they are hugely important. Rather, the first three are more introductory, if you like, and thus require more time.

First, God provides for partakers of the age to come in our utter transformation in anticipation of the end. Ephesians 2:1–10 shows us this. In this passage, we are reminded that we were dead in our transgressions and sins and were all by nature children of wrath. That is, we were not merely out of sorts with ourselves or suffering the inevitable consequences of moral decay. Rather, we were actually standing judicially under God's wrath and sentence of death. But because of his great love for us, God, who is rich in mercy, made us alive with Christ. God provides for our utter transformation out of sheer grace, received through faith alone. This whole salvation is itself a gift from God.

But it's not just a matter of getting a certain status, of simply being right with God and declared righteous in his eyes, even though it is scarcely imaginable that anything could be more wonderful that that! But God's provision is even richer than that, for he transforms us into those who do good works. It's true that we are saved by faith alone, but genuine faith, as the Reformers used to say, is never alone.

In the second place, God creates a new humanity in anticipation of the end. We see this in Ephesians 2:11–21. The particular focus here is on Jews and Gentiles. All kinds of cultural barriers between the two have existed, but now one new humanity has been brought into existence. This theme is seen elsewhere in the New Testament. We are given a panoramic view of the ultimate new humanity, with men and women drawn from every tongue and tribe and people and nation. All gather around the throne on the last day.

In the past, I had the privilege of working with the World Evangelical Fellowship, and I presently work with the Gospel Coalition, so I seem to get around to a few countries. The diversity of heights and weights, and colors, and cultural forms is great. I keep traveling and keep "sticking my foot in it," as the saying goes. Wherever I go, I manage to break some local taboo.

But others break mine as well. For instance, in Australia no ten-year-old addresses me as "Dr. Carson"; rather, they call me "Don." But in China, no one would dare refer to me as anything less than "professor" or "doctor." I am not saying that one is better than the other. I am just saying that these kinds of things reflect different cultures and how they do things. But all of us are, in Christ, seen as one new humanity. This is secured by Christ, and already it is started. That is what the church is about. It is also why racism is so repulsive in the New Testament; we are a new humanity: men and women drawn from every tongue and tribe and people and nation, born again with a common anchoring in Christ on the cross. He creates a new humanity in anticipation of the end.

Third, God provides for the partakers of the age to come in that he discloses his concealed purposes in anticipation of the end. We see this in Ephesians 3:1–13. Paul begins with a sentence that he doesn't finish. In fact, he picks it up again further on in verse 14. But Paul begins this way: "For this reason I, Paul, a prisoner for Christ Jesus on behalf of you Gentiles—". Paul is almost certainly dictating, and, borne along by the Spirit, he remembers that there is something else he wants to say before he takes that thought to its conclusion in verse 14. First he pauses and says, in effect, "Surely you have heard about the administration of God's grace that was given to me for you, that is, regarding the mystery made known to me by revelation, as I have already written briefly." Paul is telling these people that as they read this letter they will be able to understand his insight into the mystery of Christ, which was not made known to people in other generations as it has now been revealed by the Spirit to God's holy apostles and prophets.

The word *mystery* is used some twenty-seven or twenty-eight times in the New Testament. In almost every instance, it does not mean *mystery* in the sense that we talk about a "thriller" or a "whodunit." Rather, the term, as Paul uses it, regards mysteriousness as referring to the final incomprehensibility of God. Very simply, *mystery* refers to what God has kept secret in the past, but has now revealed.

Now let me step aside from the text for a moment and address something in contemporary evangelicalism. At the risk of making a huge overgeneralization, I will say that those from the dispensational end of eschatology constantly talk about what is "new" in the new covenant. Those of us from the Reformed tradition tend to talk about all the continuities between the old and new covenants. So we must avoid playing up what is new to the exclusion of the continuity it has with the old. The Scriptures insist that although these things have been hidden, they have not been hidden absolutely. They are there in the text, but people didn't see them.

Let me give a few examples. Think of the Passover sacrifice—before Jesus came, how many people saw that the ultimate Passover would be the Lamb hanging on a cross, signifying that God's wrath passed over his own people? Or consider Yom Kippur, the Day of Atonement. On that day, the high priest would enter the Most Holy Place with the blood of sacrifice. How many people saw that Jesus would be the ultimate high priest, that his blood would be taken before the heavenly tabernacle, to use the language of the author of Hebrews? And again and again, as we move from the old covenant to the new, we are reminded how people did not see that which we claim is actually there in the Scriptures.

But it goes further. Even Jesus' own band of apostles had trouble with this. For example, after Jesus had died and was buried, the apostles themselves were not in the upstairs room saying, "I can hardly wait till Sunday!" Why not? Hadn't Jesus told them again and again that he would rise again? But you know what they were thinking, perhaps: "There's another deep, enigmatic utterance from the Master." They didn't have a clue, and yet the New Testament writers show us passage after passage in the Old Testament that anticipates a crucified and resurrected Messiah. But it is all in veiled language, typological language, a language of patterns and types. It's there, but you don't see it until after the coming and glory of Christ.

Let me also briefly address another contemporary issue on which there is some confusion. It relates directly to what we have been studying. As you read the Bible carefully, and you come across a passage in the New Testament that quotes the Old Testament, you may take the time to look up the Old Testament passage. But upon finding it, you sometimes think, "Good grief, what's going on here? I don't see how Paul got that from that!"

Now, I have devoted a lot of the last thirty years of my life to addressing precisely those kinds of questions. When I first began, I wondered to myself how I would have done it, if I had been organizing the Bible. And, in my arrogance, I thought maybe Isaiah 53 should sound something like this: "And it shall come to pass in those days, says the Lord, that there shall be a Roman emperor by the name of Caesar Augustus." Then I would place this in a footnote: "Yes, I know we are still in the grip of the Assyrians. But after these Assyrians come the Babylonians, and after the Babylonians come the Medo-Persians, and after that the Greeks. Eventually what are now seven little villages on the left bank of the Tiber will come together and form the city of Rome, and the Romans will beat up the Greeks and what is left of their empire. The particular Roman ruler that I am talking about is Caesar Augustus, but this is about seven hundred years down the track." I would here direct the reader back to the main text, and have the prophet say something like, "And this Caesar shall issue a decree that the entire Roman world should be enrolled." Then I would unpack the whole biblical narrative, naming dates and places and times and so on.

Now, wouldn't that be great prophecy? Who could deny its truth at this point, with every little detail named seven hundred years in advance? Mind you, across those seven hundred years there would be many parents who would name their daughter Mary, and many boys with the name of Joseph running around. And if Pilate actually came on the scene and had some knowledge of the specific prediction concerning him, I can imagine him saying, "I will not wash my hands!" What then?

103

Well, then God's prophecy would fail. My point is simply that the fulfillment of prophecy would actually be more difficult under such circumstances.

But, in fact, God has, through the prophets, predicted many of the crucial things about Christ and his coming and everything else, but in his infinite wisdom he has done so through types, patterns, dynasties, events, and sacrificial systems. And in our moral blindness, in our decay, in our folly, in our inability to see how wonderful this all is, we did not see. But now, in the fullness of time, God has disclosed the mystery in Christ. So when the apostles preached, they did not say, "Well, you have to wait around and have a private revelation." What they did say was, "Go back to the Scriptures. If you understand them properly, you will see that it is actually there." Again and again, they point to the Scriptures. The whole Bible has a deep continuity, embedded right in the structure of everything.

Now, to return to where we left off: Paul tells the Ephesians that they have heard about the administration of God's grace that was given to him for them; that is, the mystery made known to him by revelation, as he has already written briefly. Amongst the things thus disclosed was the coming together of Jews and Gentiles in one body. All the pieces were there to see this coming; after all, already in the Abrahamic covenant there was the promise of a seed through which all the nations of the earth would be blessed. Now this is unpacked in its fullness. God creates a new humanity in anticipation of the end.

Fourth, God does more than we ask or imagine and thereby elicits prayer from us in anticipation of the end. We see this in Ephesians 3:14–21. This is a prayer that God would work in us to make us grow in holiness and in depth of appreciation for his love for us, because we cannot be mature without such increasing depth of appreciation of his love for us. A child tends to be emotionally secure when he comes from a family that is full of love. In the same way, we must grow in our appreciation of God's love for us. Paul's prayer ends with the words, "Now to him who is able to do far more abundantly than all that we ask or think, according to the power at work within us" (3:20). God has promised to do more than we ask or imagine.

Fifth, God builds truth and unity into his body in anticipation of the end. I think this theme runs all the way through from 4:1 to 6:9. There God tells us in practical passage after practical passage that, for the partakers of the age to come, how you live, how you speak, how you love, how you deny yourself—all of this is in anticipation of what will be on the last day. And yet at the same time we still remain in this old age; we still remain in this dying age. We are living in the last days (Paul could say this when he was writing!), and because of this we will be in conflict.

Thus, sixth and finally, God equips and arms his people in anticipation of the end. So we are told in 6:10–20. The devil is filled with rage because he knows his time is short, as Revelation 12 tells us. We are still going to struggle. And Paul says our struggle is not against human beings. It is not against flesh and blood, so you don't win this struggle with carbine rifles. No, our struggle is against the rulers and authorities in the heavenly places, the spiritual forces of evil. Therefore, put on the full armor of God, which he so richly provides to his saints, as he equips and arms his people in anticipation of the end.

When you read the biblical story line and unpack it, you discover that from the fall onward there are certain descriptors of our condition. On the one hand, we are guilty before God and have attracted his curse. This calls for a solution. We ourselves have become corrupted. We have lost our relationship with God, and we are under sentence of death. And out of our broken relationships, because of *the* broken relationship with our Creator, come bitterness and hate and rape and war and all the rest. And as if this weren't enough, the entire created order is under the same curse, sentenced to death and not operating as it ought.

But, in closing, we must see that the salvation that God has brought us in Christ Jesus addresses all of what I just mentioned. In justification, we are brought back to and accepted by God. He declares us just, not because we are, but because Christ has borne our sins in his body on the tree. But he has given us more than justification. He has given us new birth, made us the sons of the living God, with the power of God already pulsating within us to transform us. Not only so, we are pressing on toward the climax of all things; the entire created order groans in travail, waiting for the final adoption. Paul tells us here that already we have been made partakers of the age to come. Thus, we must be anticipating the future, hungry to join the church in every generation when it says and has said, "Yes, even so, come quickly Lord Jesus" (cf. Rev. 22:20).

7

The Four Main
Millennial Views

CORNELIS P. VENEMA

And he seized the dragon, that ancient serpent,
who is the devil and Satan, and bound him for a
thousand years. (Revelation 20:2)

IN THIS CHAPTER, we are going to examine the four
main millennial views. We are not going to look at all the varia-
tions that one finds within these particular views, but rather get
a broad overview of each one. When we speak of "millennial
views," we are describing the various approaches to the millennium, or the thousand years, of Revelation 20. This chapter will
not be an exegesis of that chapter; rather, it will explain how
Christians have historically viewed the millennium.

I want to approach these four main views by giving you a sense of when each view was prominent in the history of the church. I also want to examine some of the distinguishing features of each view. I will not be able to avoid some commentary, which may sound a bit prejudicial. But that is not my primary interest. I have frequently been asked what these views have in common. It is a great question, because it is ultimately a question to which we need to come at the end of the day.

Also, by way of introduction, since these views can cause so much heated debate, let me suggest that everyone who interacts with another's view on this topic strive for balance. While there may be some significant issues at stake, they are not as large as, say, whether God exists, or Jesus Christ as the eternal Son become man for us and our salvation, or other fundamental articles of the faith.

Two Categories of Millennial Views

It helps to begin by recognizing that these four views really fall into just two categories, with two views in each category. The first two views, broadly speaking, may be labeled as premillennial. These views regard the millennium that John saw in the vision of Revelation 20 as a period in redemptive history that will follow the return of Christ at the end of the age. These views (again, broadly speaking) teach that when Christ comes and puts his enemies under his feet, then those who come with him and those who are upon the earth as believers will be raised in resurrection glory. They will then reign with Christ upon the earth for a period of one thousand years. Thus, these views are properly called premillennial.

There are two premillennial views. They are so named because they both teach that Christ returns prior to (hence, the "pre" affixed to the term) the commencement of the millennium. The older of the two views is called historic premillennialism. The other is more recent, though many of its proponents would argue that it is the truly historic view. It is called dispensational premillennialism. These are the two dominant premillennial views.

Then there are the two postmillennial views. At this point, we get into a little difficulty with terminology because one of the two postmillennial views is called postmillennialism. Some readers may be scratching their heads already! But, broadly speaking, any view is properly considered postmillennial which regards the coming of Christ as occurring "post," or after, the millennium of Revelation 20. The two views in this category, called postmillennialism and amillennialism, disagree on their understanding of the millennial kingdom, but both agree that Christ's coming at the end of this age will be after the millennium. In either scheme, the only thing that follows our Lord's coming after the millennium is the age to come—the final state, the eternal kingdom, the new heavens and the new earth, wherein dwells righteousness.

Historic Premillennialism

Those are the two main categories in which we can put all four millennial views. But let us examine the actual views themselves, individually. We will start with the premillennial views, the first of which I have denominated *historic premillennialism*. Historic premillennialism gets its name because in the early church, among the church fathers (from the second through roughly the fifth century), this was the dominant view. Hence, it is called "historic." Some go so far as to argue (I don't think correctly) that it was really the only position on the question that existed in the early church. But it definitely had many exponents in the early church, boasting such names as Irenaeus, Tertullian, and Athanasius.

During the Middle Ages, and until the time of the Reformation, historic premillennialism tended to recede as the dominant view in the church. This happened largely through the influence of figures like Augustine, who argued that the millennium of Revelation 20 was really describing the age of the church between the time of Christ's first and second comings. To be sure, though, historic premillennialism had its proponents during both the Middle Ages and the Reformation.

This view enjoyed some resurgence in the middle and latter parts of the twentieth century—and on into the twenty-first century—thanks to a number of evangelical New Testament scholars, such as George Eldon Ladd. In fact, the movement known as progressive dispensationalism is arguably a move on the part of some dispensationalists in the direction of historic premillennialism, away from some of the distinctive features of dispensationalism. So historic premillennialism (whether in its common form or as progressive dispensationalism) is becoming, in many respects, a rather popular position today. You will find it among Christians who take the Scriptures seriously and believe the Bible to be God's very words.

What about the position itself? Again, just to sketch out the details: premillennialists understand the millennium as a literal, thousand-year period of time, during which the kingship of our Lord Jesus Christ is manifested in a way that now (at least to the eye that does not believe) remains hidden. There are a couple of distinctives relating to historic premillennialism to keep in mind, especially concerning what we may call "the signs of the times." These are those events that our Lord delineates in places like Matthew 24, which express opposition to Christ, his gospel, and the coming of his kingdom. Jesus tells us there that the love of many will grow cold, that many will apostatize, or fall away, and that there will be false christs.

One of the main differences between historic premillennialists and dispensational premillennialists is that the latter are either "pre-" or "post-tribulation" in regard to the so-called rapture of the church. Historic premillennialists would be labeled as "post-tribulationalists"; that is, they believe that in a discourse like Matthew 24, when our Lord speaks of the signs of the times, mentioning things like tribulation and affliction, he is referring to a time prior to the millennial age, when the church will experience intensified opposition, trials, persecution, and affliction. Hence, historic premillennialists would say that Jesus comes after these things. Dispensational premillennialists are divided, but most would say that Christ returns before they take place.

A few other distinctives about historic premillennialism need to be mentioned. Most historic premillennialists believe that when Paul says in Romans 11:26 that "all Israel will be saved," he is referring to the nation of Israel. They believe this will happen just prior to the return of Christ. Historic premillennialists teach that the ethnic Israelites will be grafted into the same olive tree, and so be numbered among the one people of God, composed of Jewish and Gentile believers alike, all of whom constitute the church of the Lord Jesus Christ. This way of thinking clearly distinguishes historic premillennialists from their dispensationalist cousins. Historic premillennialists maintain the unity of the one people of God (being the church), but they do reserve a place for a future conversion of many—not all, but many—from among God's ancestral people Israel.

111

Before we move on, let me say a word about the purpose of the millennium in this scheme. According to historic premillennialism, the millennium is the time when the great Old Testament promises of peace and prosperity for the people of God are fulfilled. The millennial age will be a period of the administration of justice, of wonderful blessing under the gospel rule and reign of Christ upon the earth.

Dispensational Premillennialism

We now move on to dispensational premillennialism, or *dispensationalism*. What we have said so far may seem rather rudimentary and easy to understand, in comparison to the complexities that accompany dispensational premillennialism! How is it distinguished from historic premillennialism? Again, let us begin with a little history.

Dispensational premillennialism has its roots in a revival that took place in England in the nineteenth century. This revival produced the English Brethren, the primary figure of which was John Nelson Darby. His teaching in the area of eschatology was popularized by the Scofield Reference Bible, which was first published in 1909. The notes for that study Bible were written by Cyrus I. Scofield. With the publication of his study Bible (which was revised—some would say toned down—in 1967), he became the principal exponent and author of some of the most distinctive and abiding features of dispensational premillennialism. We can roughly say that dispensationalism began in England and came to North America via the notes of Cyrus Scofield's study Bible. It has been widely used and distributed ever since.

Dispensationalism tends to be a more North American expression of premillennialism than any of the other views. I don't say that to demean dispensationalists, but only to alert them that those who share their views in other parts of the world (say, Scotland) may not have been tutored by the Scofield Reference Bible, and thus may not be entirely privy to certain things that American dispensationalists take for granted.

I have a somewhat personal stake in these discussions. As a young man in California, I attended an ardently dispensational school for three years. There I was, a Reformed minister's son, who thought that what my father taught was what the Bible, in fact, taught. We held (and I still do) a very high view of Scripture. We believed every word of the Bible; in fact, one of our confessions says that we believe "without a doubt all things contained therein." So I thought I was a Bible-believing Christian, by anyone's account.

However, I was accused at that school of being an unbeliever, as far as much of what the Scriptures taught, because I didn't hold to some of the distinctives of dispensational premillennialism! I must admit—and this is not a criticism of my father—that I had never even heard of dispensationalism. By this personal anecdote and my previous mention of the American character of modern dispensationalism, I am only attempting to illustrate that it has not been the more predominant view in the history of the church.

Since the early twentieth century, however, dispensational premillennialism has spread elsewhere through evangelistic and missionary efforts. In fact, I think one the positive qualities of dispensational premillennialism is that its adherents tend to be very zealous about gospel proclamation, missionary efforts, and evangelism. This is not to be despised, but to be recognized for what it is genuinely worth.

Again, though, dispensational premillennialism has been primarily a North American development. One leading proponent in the twentieth century was J. Dwight Pentecost. Another was Hal Lindsey, who popularized this system of thought with his best-selling book from the 1970s, *The Late, Great Planet Earth*. In addition to these influential figures are a number of seminaries that consider themselves dispensational premillennialist; perhaps the most prominent is Dallas Theological Seminary.

Before we leave our historical survey, we should make note of one more interesting detail. One of the major intramural discussions taking place today among those who subscribe to this view has to do with whether or not Calvinism is compatible with this system. Historically, there have been many prominent Calvinists (at least soteriologically) who espoused dispensationalism, such as Donald Grey Barnhouse, the pastor of historic Tenth Presbyterian Church in Philadelphia during the early part of the twentieth century. In recent times, though he is not quite as outspoken as others, John MacArthur is perhaps the preeminent example of this phenomenon.

We now turn to examine the distinctives of dispensational premillennialism. These are very complex, but the main distinctive of dispensationalism over against historic premillennialism is the view that God has two distinct peoples. He has an earthly people, Israel, with whom, in Abraham, he made an unconditional covenant. He promised him a progeny and a land, and, later, a king who would sit upon his father's throne, the throne of King David. So, according to dispensational premillennialism, God has an earthly people, Israel, to whom he makes distinct promises that are likewise earthly and appertain to Israel distinctly.

But God also has a spiritual people, who are predominantly Gentile, being gathered during this dispensation of the church. This has been going on since Christ's first coming. More specifically, this has been going on since Pentecost and will continue until the time of the rapture. The fundamental claim of the dispensationalists is, then, that God is gathering throughout history, not one people, but two peoples. Furthermore, with respect to these two peoples, he makes distinct arrangements, with particular promises for each of them. In the one case, he makes earthly promises; in the other case, spiritual promises. His people who are earthly and material receive earthly, material promises; his people who are spiritual and heavenly receive spiritual, heavenly promises.

In the dispensational system, one approaches the Word of God and finds there that history is divided into a number of dispensations. This language of "dispensations" comes from a Greek word that is often translated "dispensational economy." It has reference to the way you manage your household or administer the affairs of your household. God is the great housekeeper and steward of all creation and history. Throughout the history of redemption, he has distinctly arranged his relationships with those whom he seeks to redeem by differing household arrangements, or dispensations. This is how he would realize his redemptive purpose with respect to them.

One does not want to get lost in all of this because, although both classic dispensationalism and premillennial dispensationalism distinguish seven dispensations, in the latter scheme the dispensations that really matter are twofold. They are the dispensation of the law under Moses with respect to Israel and the dispensation through Christ and particularly by his apostles—especially Paul—of the gospel to the Gentiles in this present age. In the gospel age, according to this teaching, we are no longer under the law, but under grace.

This arrangement raises an interesting question regarding dispensationalism: are dispensationalists actually saying that these different arrangements are, in fact, different ways whereby

God provides for the salvation of his people? In answering this question, it would be unfair and incorrect to say that dispensationalists today teach that there are other ways of salvation or a distinct way of salvation for the Jewish people whom God saves. One need only read the Dallas Statement of Faith to see that such is not the case; it clearly states that there is but one mediator between God and man, one whose blood can ultimately wash away the guilt and pollution of our sin and so on, and that is Jesus Christ alone. But the impression is certainly given, especially among older writers within dispensationalism, that God had a program of salvation so radically different for Israel that he would save them by means other than the manner in which he saves his spiritual people, the predominantly Gentile church.

The way this works itself out in terms of dispensational teaching is that the promises made in the Old Testament, because they were made to Israel, do not pertain to the church. The church, in God's purposes of grace with respect to the salvation of the Gentiles, represents, from the vantage point of Old Testament promises, a mystery that was not made known or revealed. This was so because it was not pertinent to God's purposes with respect to his Old Testament people Israel.

The Gospels, in this framework, are usually presented as teaching that Christ came initially to his own in order to realize and effect the promises that had been made to Old Testament Israel. Christ would literally sit upon the throne of his father David and establish the kingdom that he had promised, with the millennium commencing after this. But Israel refused to receive him as the promised Messiah, whereupon God gave his attention to the Gentiles. This he made known subsequent to the death, resurrection, and ascension of Christ and the outpouring of the Holy Spirit, especially through the apostle Paul. This was God's purpose in this age: the present gospel age, this "time between the times," is a parenthesis within God's historic purposes for Israel. Some dispensationalists actually call the church age an interruption—an insertion into the calendar, where God dispenses with his direct dealings with Israel in order to take up and address himself to his purposes now revealed. These had previously been hidden, but the mystery of the gospel has now come to the fore; that is, that the Gentiles, his spiritual people, should be saved through the ministry of the gospel in the church age.

We must note, as well, two important aspects of premillennial dispensationalism. These are the millennium of Revelation 20 and something known as the rapture, which is related to a certain exegesis of Daniel 9:24–27. The basic question is how will God, who has interrupted his fulfillment of literal promises to the literal people of Israel for the sake of the gathering of the Gentile church in this dispensation of the church age, get back on track, so to speak? I don't mean to use that language pejoratively at all; the question is a valid one.

At this point, one must understand why the rapture plays such a significant role for contemporary, as well as classic, dispensationalists. First Thessalonians 4:15–17 is said to refer to Christ coming for his saints before the tribulations of the end. This will occur with a pretribulational rapture. There is nothing on the prophetic calendar having forewarned its sudden coming: no tribulation, no emerging Antichrist, no man of lawlessness, no cooling off of the love of many—nothing about an intense persecution and trial for the people of God that would need to occur prior to the rapture. Rather, it is sudden, secret, and unexpected. Its purpose is quite literally to snatch up the church to meet Christ in the air, and there to enjoy the marriage feast of the Lamb mentioned in Revelation 19. This feast will last for seven years.

Daniel 9:24–27 speaks of seventy weeks: sixty-two weeks, then another seven weeks, and then the seventieth week. The church age comes in between the sixty-ninth and seventieth week. This seventieth week also follows the rapture of the Gentile church. Christ then comes, not "for" his saints, but "with" his saints at the end of a seven-year period of tribulation, which will include great tribulation and the emergence of the Antichrist, during which time the gospel will be preached in a particular way to Jewish people. They will then turn in faith to God in great numbers, and be brought into the kingdom. Christ will come at the end of that seven-year period. The millennium of Revelation, a period of literally one thousand years, will then commence. During this time, the promises made to David, Israel, and Abraham will literally be fulfilled in terms of an actual land flowing with milk and honey and the enjoyment of prosperity. Essentially, all of the great prophetic promises will literally come to pass.

Remember, this is the roughest of sketches; I can't possibly do justice in the space remaining to the details involved in this view. But the purpose of the millennium is to fulfill the literal promise of the conferral of a literal kingdom to a literal king upon a literal throne in a literal land for Israel. Indeed, in the more radical expressions of classic dispensationalism, it is actually taught that God's two peoples will live in separate "places" in the millennial kingdom. The Gentile church will be the heavenly people in the new heavens. Israel will be the earthly people on the new earth. This strikes me as very different from the language of Jerusalem "coming down out of heaven" (Rev. 21:2), with heaven and earth reconciled and joined together. Further, John pictures for us at the end of the Bible the people of God from all the tribes, tongues, peoples, and nations of the earth—all of them, Jew and Gentile alike—dwelling together in one household, in one new heavens and earth, where any disjunction or separation between the two is done away with.

Let me make one final note on dispensational premillennialism before we move on to other views. One of its characteristic features is the claim that this position necessarily follows if you read the Bible "literally." Those who hold other views will be accused of "spiritualizing" the meaning of many passages of Scripture, thus depriving them of their literal meaning. This literalism is required by the dispensational premillennialist system.[1]

Postmillennialism

If our study of dispensationalism has thoroughly confused you, the good news is that the two postmillennial views are much simpler. Remember, we classified both amillennialism and postmillennialism proper as postmillennial because both place the return of Christ after the millennium of Revelation 20.

We will begin with *postmillennialism* proper. This view has flourished more within Reformed and Presbyterian circles than anywhere else. For example, those who taught at "Old Princeton" were predominantly postmillennial. It distinguishes itself from its amillennial cousin with the teaching of a coming "golden age." This term refers to a certain point when, through gospel preaching and the work of the Spirit by means of the gospel, the kingship of our Lord Jesus Christ and the discipleship of the nations will prevail to such an extent that we will enter into a distinct period of prosperity and blessing, following from the Bible's promise of universal covenant blessing. Some postmillennialists

1. Editor's note: For a thorough discussion of the dispensational approach to literal interpretation, see Vern S. Poythress, *Understanding Dispensationalism* (Phillipsburg, NJ: P&R, 1993).

teach that this will occur rather quickly through a great revival granted by a fresh outpouring of the Holy Spirit; others speak of it happening in a more progressive fashion, through extended gospel preaching and missionary endeavor.

Broadly speaking, there are two kinds of golden age postmillennialists. There is the older kind, represented today by Iain Murray, which we could call the "Puritan variety," since many of the Puritans were golden age postmillennialists. Then there is today the "theonomic" or "reconstructionist" version of postmillennialism, perhaps best represented by the likes of Douglas Wilson. Both look for a golden age, but what distinguishes reconstructionists from the classic or Puritan variety of postmillennialism is their belief that the civil authorities play an instrumental role in the realization of God's kingdom purposes for the golden age millennium. Their program also includes Christianization and the use of state authority in the enforcement of the law of Christ and its sanctions. Reconstructionists want to take the Old Testament case law, with all of its sanctions, and apply it to the modern state. They will speak sometimes of a "Christian" state.

What follows is, like our examination of the other views, merely a brief sketch. There is much more that could be said about postmillennialism. The important thing to note is that Christ comes after the millennium, on this scheme. The millennium is construed as a golden age of unprecedented blessings, brought about by the preaching of the gospel and the discipleship of the nations.

Amillennialism

I will conclude our (necessarily brief) overview with *amillennialism*. The term itself is subject to much confusion. It does not mean "no millennium," as the name might suggest. Rather, it takes the thousand years of Revelation 20 as figurative, rather than literal. In this way, it agrees with postmillennialism proper.

The amillennial position, from a historical point of view, rose to prominence in the church with Augustine in roughly the fifth century. Thereafter, it continued to be the view that one comes across frequently in both the Roman Catholic and Eastern Orthodox communions. In the course of history, both of these groups, in amillennial fashion, considered the millennium of Revelation 20, broadly speaking, to be identical with the age of the church. During this period, the church has been given the Spirit to empower God's people to prosecute his purposes effectively for the redemption of his people through the means that he has given to the church. So, if you include those in the communions of Roman Catholicism and Eastern Orthodoxy, amillennialism is clearly the predominant view throughout history. Furthermore, I think it has been the majority opinion within Reformed and Presbyterian churches as well.

On this view, the millennium of Revelation 20 is a great picture of how, during this age, Satan has been prevented and is prevented by the coming of Christ from deceiving the nations totally any longer. He has been cast down from heaven to the earth. The Devil cannot prevent Christ from gathering to himself his rightful inheritance, which are the nations that the Father has promised to him. So, very simply, we are living in the millennium right now.

One thing that we should address is the teaching of two resurrections in Revelation 20. Revelation 20:4–6 reads:

> Then I saw thrones, and seated on them were those to whom the authority to judge was committed. Also I saw the souls of those who had been beheaded for the testimony of Jesus and

for the word of God, and who had not worshiped the beast or its image and had not received its mark on their foreheads or their hands. They came to life and reigned with Christ for a thousand years. The rest of the dead did not come to life until the thousand years were ended. This is the first resurrection. Blessed and holy is the one who shares in the first resurrection! Over such the second death has no power, but they will be priests of God and of Christ, and they will reign with him for a thousand years.

What is John referring to here in this language of "the first resurrection" and "the second death"? Premillennialists tend to argue that John is here referring to a bodily resurrection when he speaks of the first resurrection. This view, I think, flattens the language of resurrection in the New Testament, insisting that "coming to life" and "resurrection" always and without exception refer to bodily resurrection. I don't think that is the case.

"The first resurrection" likely refers to the life and blessing reserved for the saints, especially those who have died and will be raised on the last day. Thus, it is not a physical resurrection, but a spiritual participation in Christ. John sees this particularly to be the case for martyred saints. But it also refers to all who are united to Christ. They enjoy particular and pronounced blessings because of their union with Christ.

What about "the second death"? This, too, has reference to a spiritual, not physical, circumstance. The "rest of the dead" are the wicked and unbelieving. Since they were not spiritually resurrected, they will not enjoy the blessings of God forever. Rather, they are subject not only to physical death (as are all people), but to eternal death ("the second death"), separated from God's presence of blessing.

Thus, in the amillennial view, this important chapter offers us a behind-the-scenes glimpse of the continuing triumph of the Lamb, as he gathers his elect from the nations. They are already enjoying God's blessing in their lives, even if they are called to suffer persecution or martyrdom. This would have been tremendously encouraging for the first readers of the book of Revelation.

Revelation 20 should also encourage us today. When we see so many things so terribly wrong in this world, we are called upon to remember who is in control. We are called to live our lives as those who have been blessed with participation in the first resurrection. And we are called to live in hope, knowing that Satan is bound, that his time is short, and that Christ will triumph.

8

A Pastoral Guide to Life after Death

RICHARD D. PHILLIPS

Even though I walk through the valley of the shadow of death, I will fear no evil, for you are with me.
(Psalm 23:4)

DEATH IS A SUBJECT that most of us spend little time thinking about. As a pastor, I do not have that luxury, for I am around dying people often. This causes me to think about what I have learned in my ministry to dying people.

One of the most important lessons I have learned is that I do not need to present the latest scholarly exegesis on a particular passage of Scripture to dying saints. Rather, the well-worn paths of the familiar text are what people facing death most need. My

125

favorite passage for helping someone come to grips with death, though certainly not the only one, is Psalm 23, which begins:

> The LORD is my shepherd; I shall not want.
>> He makes me lie down in green pastures.
> He leads me beside still waters.
>> He restores my soul.
> He leads me in paths of righteousness
>> for his name's sake.

These verses picture a believer like a sheep following the shepherd. It is a wonderful depiction of how the Lord, our Shepherd, cares for us in this life—and in death. Then we get to verse 4, which, I think, must be quoted in the King James Version: "Yea, though I walk through the valley of the shadow of death, I will fear no evil: for thou art with me; thy rod and thy staff they comfort me."

The first point to make from these verses is that for a believer, death is not at the end, but it is in the middle. Death is not something *into which* we go, but something *through which* we pass. This is not normally how we think about either death in general or this psalm in particular.

Typically, we look upon our lives as bounded by a sort of dark line (death itself), and then there's the end—but not according to David in the Twenty-third Psalm. Death is in the middle of the psalm, and what comes afterward is glorious.

This sentiment was vividly illustrated by Dr. James M. Boice, late pastor of the historic Tenth Presbyterian Church in Philadelphia. I had the privilege of being close to him when he was dying. Part of his amazing example was that it seemed that he was only just beginning to live when he died. He was not looking back with regret but forward with anticipation. This should be the impression that people get around dying Christians: saints are only just beginning to live when they are dying!

The Biblical View of Death

Since we are studying death and dying, our first and best question is this: what does the Bible say about death? In the first place, we should note that the Bible acknowledges *the reality of death*. This runs against the grain of a culture today that wants to sugarcoat death, by saying things like "He passed away." The simple reality is that phrases like this are not Christian. I force myself to say "He has died" or "She is dead." As believers, we have to face the reality of death. This is simply to speak biblically: "It is appointed for man to die once, and after that comes judgment" (Heb. 9:27).

You may be familiar with the famous resolutions of Jonathan Edwards, the majority of which he wrote at age nineteen. One of them was this: "Resolved, to think much on all occasions of my own dying and of the common circumstances which attend death."[1] What he meant was that our bodies are going to decompose. And, at age nineteen, Jonathan Edwards said, "I want to live as someone who lives in light of that." To say that that kind of thinking is foreign to most modern people, never mind nineteen-year-olds, would be a great understatement. But in Edwards's world, death was never far away from anyone. This is not the case for most of us today, and so we sugarcoat it.

I can relate to Edwards in some ways. As a pastor, I am often around death. Before being called to the ministry, however, I was an army officer for thirteen years. There, too, I saw a lot

1. Jonathan Edwards, *Jonathan Edwards' Resolutions and Advice to Young Converts*, ed. Stephen J. Nichols (Phillipsburg, NJ: P&R Publishing, 2001), 18.

of death. So, in many ways, I've seen much more death than the average person. But what is interesting to me is that death affects me now much more than it used to. Although I've been around death so much, and seen my share of dead bodies, I find myself thinking more and more, "You know, Rick, it really will not be that long until your lifeless body is lying there." We would all do well to heed Edwards's advice and resolve to think much on all occasions of our own dying. So Christians are to acknowledge the reality of death; it is really unhelpful for us not to do so.

In the second place, we must recognize *the wrongness of death*. Forrest Gump, that mediocre theologian, expressed the sentiments of most people when, repeating his mother's words, he said, "Dyin's just a part of livin'." This is profoundly wrong. But this kind of falsehood is not limited to Hollywood. It has found its way into Christian circles as well.

Consider a teaching that is, sadly, becoming more and more accepted by evangelicals. I am thinking of what is known as theistic evolution. One of the reasons why we should reject this teaching is that theistic evolution is a process in which the creative engine is death. And if, in Genesis 1, after beholding what he has created and pronouncing it "very good" (Gen. 1:31), God is describing a process of natural selection that includes death, then God is pronouncing death to be very good. But the Bible does not look upon death and say it is good. Just the opposite is the case, in fact. The Bible teaches that death is the result of sin, of something evil and corrupt (Gen. 2:17; Rom. 5:12–14). Death is so wrong that Paul says, "the last enemy to be destroyed is death" (1 Cor. 15:26).

The Lord Jesus Christ himself took death seriously and considered it seriously wrong. For example, in John 11:1–44, the apostle narrates for us the inspired history of the resurrection of one of Jesus' friends, Lazarus. We see our Lord taking death seriously in the shortest verse of the New Testament, verse 35, which reads, "Jesus wept."

Now bear in mind that Jesus knew his friend was going to die. In fact, when he was told that Lazarus was sick, Jesus stayed where he was two days longer (v. 6). When he did show up at Bethany, as he stood outside his friend's tomb, knowing full well that in a brief moment his friend would be alive again, what did the Lord of life do? He wept. This was not just sentimental weeping. It was frustrated anger that our Lord expressed as he wept. This is because death is offensive. It is something with which we must never be at peace.

My father died ten years ago, and I was very close to him. I will still find myself grieving unexpectedly at times. At those times, people will say to me, "When are you going to get over your father's death?" Maybe you have a child or another loved one who has died, and people will say silly things like, "You need to get over it."

My answer to such questions and statements is that I will get over my father's death at the resurrection and not one minute earlier. To be sure, the Lord will help me in my grief. But the grief is intense precisely because death is so wrong. So let us be done with such expressions as "He passed away," as if the deceased is on vacation! No, he has suffered death. He is dead. And it is a great offense. C. S. Lewis captured what I am saying when he wrote, "I'm not so much afraid of death as ashamed of it."[2] We must always be ashamed of the awful unnaturalness of death. We know we were not made for this. We know instinctively, if I can use that language, that death is an intruder that has crept in stealthily to destroy us.

2. C. S. Lewis, *God in the Dock* (Grand Rapids: Eerdmans, 1970), 150.

So we see that death is both real and unnatural. However, we must also distinguish between *the death of the righteous* and *the death of the wicked.* Robert Shaw, a Puritan minister who wrote a wonderful commentary on the Westminster Confession, said this:

> There is, indeed, a vast difference between the death of the righteous and that of the wicked. To the latter, death is the effect of the law-curse, and the harbinger of everlasting destruction; but to the former, death is . . . the termination of all sin and sorrow, and an entrance into life eternal. To them death is divested of its sting, and rendered powerless to do them any real injury. . . . It is their release from warfare, their deliverance from woe, their departure to be with Christ.[3]

This is why, I think, David wrote what he did in Psalm 23:4, which speaks of walking "through the valley of the shadow of death." Death is like a shadow for Christians. Isn't that interesting language? A shadow passes over and the sun can't be seen, but the sun is there and we know it's there. So also death is made in Christ to be merely a shadow for us.

When we think about how Christians pass *through* death on the way to glory, numerous Scriptures come to mind. Psalm 121:7–8 reads:

> The LORD will keep you from all evil;
>   he will keep your life.
> The LORD will keep
>   your going out and your coming in
>   from this time forth and forevermore.

---

3. Robert Shaw, *The Reformed Faith* (repr., Inverness: Christian Focus Publications, 1974), 400.

The psalmist is saying that, for the Christian, the Lord will preserve our lives even in death. Psalm 116:15 is another place where we find this kind of thing. There we read, "Precious in the sight of the LORD is the death of his saints."

In both of these Psalms (and in many other places in Scripture), we see what a big difference there is between the death of a believer and the death of an unbeliever. Only a believer can cry with Paul,

"O death, where is your victory?
    O death, where is your sting?"

The sting of death is sin, and the power of sin is the law. But thanks be to God, who gives us the victory through our Lord Jesus Christ. (1 Cor. 15:55–57)

Unbelievers cannot reasonably say such things.

So, as Christians, we acknowledge the reality of death. We are never reconciled to death. We know the cause of death, and we know how death is transformed for us into the gateway of life. I love how Charles Spurgeon put it once, with these words: "Death—what is it? It is the waiting room where we robe ourselves for immortality; it is the place where the body, like Esther, bathes itself in spices that it may be fit for the embrace of its Lord."[4]

The Experience of Death

Before we move on from thinking about death itself, let me address the experience of death. When I was pastoring in

4. Charles Haddon Spurgeon, *Spurgeon's Sermons* (Grand Rapids: Baker Book House, 1999), 1:229.

Florida, as soon as I arrived at the church, I learned of a deacon who had been diagnosed with throat cancer. For the next two years, I watched this man endure the cycle of chemotherapy, the cancer coming back, more chemo, remission, return, etc. Then he got a medical report saying that, though he was clean right now, the cancer was certainly going to come back. When it did, this deacon would have no recourse to more chemotherapy or radiation. He and his wife came to see me with this report. I said, "Now let's prepare you to die."

Later, after her husband had died, his wife came to see me. Concerning what I told them that day, she said, "It was a little brazen, but I think we're glad you said it." The reason I felt compelled to say what surely did, in fact, seem bold, was that I'm a minister of the gospel. And only the gospel can show us how to deal with death.

During the six months that I ministered to this man before his death, we met often. We had no other text but the Twenty-third Psalm. We would meditate on it together. We would pray about it. We would talk about it. We did this right up to the day before he died. At that time he said to me, "Pastor, I'm going to go see Jesus tomorrow, and I'm going to thank him for your ministry." Now, of course, that meant a great deal to me. But I'll never forget him asking during one of our meetings, "Pastor, what's it going to be like to die?" Like many of us, this man was scared of the actual experience of death. And, like everyone else who is asked that question, I had to say, "I don't know."

Personally, I can identify with my friend's fears. I fear death. I wonder what it will be like. I don't deny that it repulses me to think about what it will be like to experience it. In this way, we are all like sheep balking before a dark, shadowy canyon. Sheep do not like to go into places like that. So why do they go? Because the shepherd is with them. The same is true for us: Jesus will be with us in the ministry of the Holy Spirit. His rod, which is a weapon to protect, will drive off all that we fear. His staff is going to pull us through it. Yes, the Lord, our Shepherd, will be with us in the valley of death.

I suppose there is much more that we could say about death itself, but that is enough to get us started in the right direction. Let's summarize what we've learned so far about death: It is real. It is our enemy. It should be and is offensive to us. It is defeated in Christ, and Christ promises to be with us as we pass through it.

What Happens after Death

Now let us turn to answering specific questions that many Christians (indeed, all people) have about death. Surely the most popular, and least understood, is this: what happens to us after we die?

Let us begin our answer by considering what happens to our bodies when we die. The Westminster Confession of Faith is very helpful on this topic. Chapter 32, section 1, states: "The bodies of men after death return to dust and see corruption." What these Puritan ministers were rightly confessing (really, just following what the Bible makes so clear) was that, at death, the soul is separated from the body.

Again, in popular culture today, people have an expression that I do not like. They will see a corpse and say, "Well, he's not there." Now, why don't I like this way of speaking? Because our bodies, in a very important way, are us. We are not Gnostics or Platonists, who believe that the body is a prison from which the soul escapes.

133

My personal frame of reference for this is, again, my own father. He died of multiple sclerosis. In terms of how it destroys the body, this dread disease is like chopping down a big oak tree with a razor blade. Two hours after my father died, the coroner came and it was not a pretty sight. I remember standing there with the coroner, saying aloud with tears streaming down my face: "This is my father and death has taken him. But I will see this body resurrected in glory!"

There is a sense, however, in which we rightly say that a dead loved one is "not there" with the lifeless body. This is because in death our souls depart from our bodies. The soul, the conscious person, that which perceives, thinks, and experiences, is not in the body. This is what Christians ought to mean when they say, "He's not here."

When someone dies, his or her body returns to dust and sees corruption, to use Westminster's language. We see this in Scripture in verses like Acts 13:36: "For David, after he had served the purpose of God in his own generation, fell asleep and was laid with his fathers and saw corruption." In Genesis 3:19, God says to Adam, "By the sweat of your face you shall eat bread, till you return to the ground, for out of it you were taken; for you are dust, and to dust you shall return." Thus, the decomposition of the body is an effect of the fall.

But the Bible doesn't just leave us there. Again, to use the Westminster Standards, the Shorter Catechism, answer 37, says this: "Their bodies, still united to Christ, do rest in their grave until the resurrection." I love the line, "still united to Christ." This teaches the biblical truth that Christ knows where the bodies of all his people are.

As an aside, I must say that this is why the traditional Christian practice in dealing with the dead is burial and not cremation. I don't want to be overly dogmatic on this point, because many people have cremated loved ones. My own father was cremated at his request, but against my wishes. Traditionally Christians, out of a respect for the body, have buried their dead. One of the reasons for this is that, in the Old Testament, having one's bodily remains submitted to the flames did not reflect well on one's theological status! If you have a moment, let me encourage you to look up these passages: Joshua 7:25; Judges 15:6; 1 Kings 13:2; 1 Kings 16:18; 2 Kings 23:20; Isaiah 66:24. You will see what I mean about the biblical idea of cremation. Christians, looking forward to the resurrection, usually refrain from inflicting damage upon the dead body, but reverence it in burial.

We have briefly seen what happens to the bodies of the righteous when they die. But what about the souls of the righteous? Since we are all going to die sooner rather than later, unless Jesus returns first, we need to be very clear about what happens to our souls when we die. The fate of our bodies until Christ returns is clear from both Scripture and experience. However, there is much confusion about what happens to a believer's soul when he or she dies.

We return again to the Westminster Confession, 32.1: "Their souls, which neither die nor sleep, having an immortal subsistence, immediately return to God who gave them." This states, first, that the soul of a believer returns to God (see Luke 23:43; Eccl. 12:7). The Confession continues: "The souls of the righteous, being then made perfect in holiness, are received into the highest heavens, where they behold the face of God, in light and glory, waiting for the full redemption of their bodies" (see Heb. 12:23; 2 Cor. 5:1, 6, 8; Phil. 1:23; Acts 3:21; Eph. 4:10). We'll examine these verses more closely in a moment. But first, let's look at a few more questions related to what happens to believers after death.

First, does death cause an extinction of being? The answer is no. It is clear from the Bible that our souls continue to exist after death. They are disembodied, but in such a manner as to be capable of exercising those powers and faculties that are essential to them.

We see this illustrated in such passages as 1 Samuel 28:1–25, which is the story of the witch of Endor. It is highly debated whether the witch conjures up Samuel or a representation of him. In any case, Saul recognizes Samuel in his state of death. Samuel speaks. He hears. He thinks. And so after we die, our souls continue to exercise those faculties that are proper to them.

A New Testament example is found in Matthew 17:1–13, the account of Jesus on the Mount of Transfiguration. There Jesus speaks with Moses and Elijah, both of whom have been dead for quite some time! Yet their inward, conscious selves—their souls—continue to do all the things that they did on earth.

A second and not unrelated question is, What about soul sleep? The Bible often uses phrases like "He is asleep" when someone has died. We need to understand that this is a meta-phorical description of the *body*, not the *soul*. So, yes, the Bible uses the language of sleep in reference to death, but it is simply metaphorical language that describes the appearance of one's body in the state of death. It is overwhelmingly clear that our souls are fully active after death.

R. C. Sproul helpfully puts it in these terms: "The Bible teaches that we do not lose consciousness when we die. We will be in heaven, aware of Christ, aware of God, and aware of the other saints who are there. We will not be clothed with our res-urrected bodies at that point, but we will be in an intermediate state, in which the soul exists without the body."[5] So neither do we cease to exist, nor is there a soul sleep.

5. R. C. Sproul, *Truths We Confess* (Phillipsburg, NJ: P&R Publishers, 2006–2007), 3:177.

We have described what doesn't happen to a believer after death, so now let us turn to what, according to the Bible, does happen. In the first place—and this is glorious even to consider—we will be in the presence of the Lord. Second Corinthians 5:1, 6–8 says,

> For we know that if the tent, which is our earthly home, is destroyed, we have a building from God, a house not made with hands, eternal in the heavens. . . . We know that while we are at home in the body we are away from the Lord, for we walk by faith, not by sight. Yes, we are of good courage, and we would rather be away from the body and at home with the Lord.

In life, we are at home in the body and absent from the presence of God in heaven. But when we die, we are absent from the body and present with the Lord. That is why he says in Philippians 1:23, "I am hard pressed between the two. My desire is to depart and be with Christ, for that is far better." What did Jesus say to the thief on the cross? "Truly, I say to you, today you will be with me in Paradise" (Luke 23:43). So the souls of the just, those who are believers in Christ, justified by faith in him alone, depart from the body to be with the Lord.

Charles Spurgeon puts it well:

> The grave what is it? It is the bath in which the Christian puts off the clothes of the body to have them washed and cleansed. Death what is it? It is the waiting room where we robe ourselves for immortality. It is the place where the body, like Esther, bathes itself in spices so that it may be fit for the embrace of the Lord. Death is the gate of life. I will not fear then to die.[6]

6. Spurgeon, *Spurgeon's Sermons*, 1:229.

What really makes death gain is to be with Christ. This is the reason that Paul said he would rather have death if he could so choose!

So, upon death, the soul of the believer retains its natural faculties. It departs from the body and thereby is in the highest heavens in the presence of the Lord, beholding his glory. That is the next statement the Confession makes: the soul is "beholding the glory of the Lord in light and holiness." The apostle John puts it this way: "Beloved, we are God's children now, and what we will be has not yet appeared; but we know that when he appears we will be like him, because we shall see him as he is" (1 John 3:2).

I have had the privilege of preaching through the gospel of John. One of my favorite verses in that gospel is chapter 17, verse 24: "Father, I desire that they also, whom you have given me, may be with me where I am, to see my glory that you have given me because you loved me before the foundation of the world." When Jesus says, "I desire," he is not merely expressing a hope. Rather, as God the Son, he is sovereignly exercising his mediatorial office, with all the rights of his fulfilled covenant. He is declaring his sovereign will for his people. We absolutely and assuredly will be with Jesus, for whatever he desires comes to pass! We will see him in the glory of his perfect humanity, and we will also see him in the glory of his deity.

Another wonderful aspect of all this is the fact that we will be perfect in holiness when we get to heaven. Here is what the author of Hebrews says:

> But you have come to Mount Zion and to the city of the living God, the heavenly Jerusalem, and to innumerable angels in festal gathering, and to the assembly of the firstborn who are enrolled in heaven, and to God, the judge of all, and to the spirits of the righteous made perfect. (Heb. 12:22–23)

So upon our soul's entrance into heaven, we will be "made perfect."

I don't know about you, but I look forward to that because I'm a little tired of myself and my sin. I am tired of the way that temptations have a hold on my flesh. But when Satan comes to me and says, "Who are you?" I have two answers. The first is Luther's answer, found in 1 John 1:7: "The blood of Jesus his Son cleanses us from all sin." When Satan tempted Luther and accused him of his sins as with a large scroll, Luther responded by saying, "You're right—but you made a mistake. You left room at the bottom, where it will be written, 'The blood of Christ cleanses me from all my sins.'" The second response I have is, "Stick around, pal. As unlikely as I admit that it is, I am going to be perfect in holiness when Christ has completed my salvation." This is what Christ guarantees us.

If this is the joy that awaits the believer, what awaits the unbeliever? The Westminster Confession answers: "The souls of the wicked after death are cast into hell, where they remain in torment and utter darkness reserved for the judgment of the great day." So the souls of the wicked are cast into hell, tormented and in utter darkness, reserved for the judgment of the great day. We see this in such passages of Scripture as Luke 16:23–24, Acts 1:25, Judges 6 and 7, and 1 Peter 3:19, to name a few.

In *Paradise Lost,* Milton has the devil say that it is better to reign in hell than serve in heaven. Many people today seem to think that the devil does indeed reign in hell. Let me assure you, however, that nobody is reigning in hell except Christ. That's right: Christ is reigning in hell. Hell, to be sure, is utter loneliness. There is just utter darkness, but the Lord Jesus Christ is still present in all of his terrifying power.

In relation to all of this, some people may ask, What about purgatory? We must realize that the whole doctrine of purgatory flows of necessity from a Roman Catholic understanding of the doctrine of justification. In their scheme, justification is not a declaration by God that we are righteous, once for all, in his sight. Rather, it begins a process that, unless you are on the level of a Mother Teresa, will not gain you entry into heaven when you die. Rather, the fires of purgation (hence the name) will "purge" you of your remaining sin and thus fit you for heaven. But let us note well: there are no references to purgatory in any canonical book of Scripture. The author of Hebrews states the matter succinctly: "It is appointed for man to die once, and after that comes judgment" (Heb. 9:27).

Let's go now to the resurrection of the body. The resurrection is a necessary and glorious part of the gospel. Most of us have lived during the age of revivalism. What I'm thinking of is the kind of decisionism or revivalism that really has marked two hundred years of Western Christianity. Because of the influence of revivalism, we still hear things like "Christianity is just fire insurance." Christianity is that, if you want to use that kind of language, but it is not only that. When we are born again, not only are we put right with God, but we begin to experience the firstfruits of Christ's resurrection, that is, the Holy Spirit.

What does Paul say when speaking of the Spirit? He says that he wants us to understand that the power that is at work in us is like the power of the Holy Spirit when God raised Jesus from the dead (Eph. 1:19–20). The Holy Spirit is resurrection power for us now, as we are being renewed spiritually. And the resurrection, both as we have a foretaste of it now, in the ministry and in the presence of the Holy Spirit, and also as we move toward the actual restoration of all things, is absolutely central to the gospel.

But we should also note that everyone is going to be resurrected. It's not just believers who will be resurrected. Unbelievers will be resurrected to an eternal existence; for believers, it will be eternal life, but for unbelievers, it will be eternal death.

The resurrection of all persons will occur immediately after Christ's second coming. And immediately after the resurrection of all persons comes the final judgment. Passages like Matthew 25:42, John 5:28, and Acts 24:15 teach this clearly. This seems to do away with a system like premillennialism since the final judgment follows immediately upon Christ's return and not a thousand years later.

What, then, happens to believers at the resurrection of the body? The Westminster Shorter Catechism, question 38, reads, "At the resurrection, believers, being raised up in glory, shall be openly acknowledged and acquitted in the day of judgment, and be perfectly blessed in the full enjoying of God to all eternity."

At the resurrection, which takes place upon the return of Christ, all who are in him will have their resurrected bodies united to their souls, subsequently to be glorified. Paul explores this in 1 Corinthians 15:42–46:

> So is it with the resurrection of the dead. What is sown is perishable; what is raised is imperishable. It is sown in dishonor; it is raised in glory. It is sown in weakness; it is raised in power. It is sown a natural body; it is raised a spiritual body. If there is a natural body, there is also a spiritual body. Thus it is written, "The first man Adam became a living being"; the last Adam became a life-giving spirit. But it is not the spiritual that is first but the natural, and then the spiritual.

Our selfsame bodies will be raised and none other. Some of you have lost children. I personally cannot imagine the pain that you must have experienced, for I have five children of my own. I cannot think about losing any one of them. But if I did lose a child, I would not get over it until the resurrection. Pastorally, as

I have had to do, I will say to parents who stand over the bodies of dead children, or spouses standing over their dead husband or wife, "Those hands will hold your hands again!" This body in Christ will not be defeated. Satan can't have it. Death will not ultimately have it. Christ will transform it into glory.

We will also be acknowledged by Christ. Matthew 25:34 teaches us this: "Then the King will say to those on his right, 'Come, you who are blessed by my Father, inherit the kingdom prepared for you from the foundation of the world.' " Isn't this wonderful? Jesus will acknowledge us as belonging to him, as having a right to his kingdom and his glory. Notice as well that he brings us to himself—"Come, you who are blessed by my Father."

So, we will be acknowledged by Christ. But we will also be acquitted by Christ. This is a very controversial subject these days. One hears (with alarming frequency) about "a future justification according to works." Advocates of a teaching known as the New Perspective on Paul (and others) teach that while we are justified by faith now, what really determines whether we "make it" in the end is our works of obedience. They point to passages like Matthew 25 in an attempt to argue this view.

I would answer this teaching by pointing out that when Jesus returns and sits on his throne, calling the sheep and goats together, he will then separate them. When Jesus says to the sheep, "Come, you who are blessed of my Father," he will be speaking to people for whom justification is completed. Why? Because they will already have been glorified. Remember that Jesus calls his sheep *after* the resurrection and the separation of these two groups! It is not as if the destiny of either group were in doubt when Jesus speaks of the good works of his people. I admit there is a final justification in Christ, and that I have not yet been finally justified. But this will only be an outward manifestation of my justification, which is already completed. So the believers who are here pictured at the final judgment are not there to be judged. Yes, they will be acquitted, but their acquittal is not in doubt. This acquittal will be manifest in our very persons, as we will already be glorified.

We will not only be acquitted openly on that day; we will also experience the eternal enjoyment of God. Revelation 21:3–5 and 1 Thessalonians 4:17 demonstrate this point. And so for us, the future resurrection is the raising of our bodies, the glorifying of our bodies as they are reunited with our souls, the open acknowledgment that we belong to Christ, our full and final acquittal in Christ, and our being brought into the eternal enjoyment of God.

The Final Judgment

Let me make a few more points about the final judgment. It is an appointed day. No one knows the day, but God has appointed it. "God has appointed a day," says the Westminster Confession, 33.1, "wherein he will judge the world in righteousness, by Jesus Christ, to whom all power and judgment is given of the Father." God will judge the earth in the person of the God-man, in the person of his Son, who is most fitting to render perfect judgment on mankind. Both Acts 17:31 and John 5:27 teach this. So it is a fixed, appointed day.

Now regarding the judgment itself, the Westminster Confession, 33.1, says: "In which day, not only the apostate angels shall be judged, but likewise all persons that have lived upon the earth shall appear before the tribunal of Christ to give an account of their thoughts, words, and deeds; and to receive according to what they have done in the body, whether good or evil." Now didn't we just say that this judgment is not according works? Is the Confession saying something different here than what we have been saying? No. Let's look at why this is the case.

First of all, the final judgment will be a just judgment. It will be a righteous judgment. A. A. Hodge wrote, "It is a dictate of natural reason and conscience that in some way, formally or informally . . . God will call all the subjects of his moral government to an exact account for their character and actions."[7] What Hodge is saying is that it must be the case that God will call his creatures to account. It is obvious that this has not yet happened, so it will happen in the judgment after death.

Who will be the subjects of judgment? The answer is apostate angels and all persons. We see this taught in Jude 6 and Hebrews 9:27. What then is the nature of their judgment? The Confession answers: "All their thoughts, words, and deeds, what they have done in the body, whether good or evil." Ecclesiastes 12:14, Matthew 12:36, and Revelation 20:12 show us this clearly.

Now let's go back to the judgment of the righteous, who will have been glorified in their persons prior to the final judgment. Therefore, this judgment is not a judgment of condemnation for those who are in Christ. Romans 8:1 says, "There is therefore now no condemnation for those who are in Christ Jesus." And look at Revelation 20:15: "If anyone's name was not found written in the book of life, he was thrown into the lake of fire." This is a very important passage in relation to the final judgment. The apostle tells us that there are two books. If you're not in Christ, there is a book in which all of your thoughts, actions, and deeds are recorded. It is going to be an unpleasant experience. I'll say to people, when I'm trying to get them to realize the severity of

---

7. A. A. Hodge, *The Confession of Faith* (repr., Edinburgh: Banner of Truth Trust, 1958), 390.

sin, "What if someone wrote down everything you said today. Would you be willing to have it read before the congregation from the pulpit?" I don't think anyone has ever answered yes—I know I certainly wouldn't. This is one book, then, from which a group will be judged.

But doesn't the Confession clearly say that all people will give an account of their thoughts, words, and deeds? Yes, it does. But there is another book. It's called the book of life. A clear reference to this is Revelation 13:8. John is talking about the followers of the beast, and he writes that "all who dwell on earth will worship it, everyone whose name has not been written before the foundation of the world in the book of life of the Lamb that was slain." The book of life is the book of the life of Jesus Christ. You must be judged by works and by works alone in the final judgment, but if your name is in the book of life, it will not be your works by which you will be judged, but his works. Suddenly, we have nothing to fear. If your name is written in the book of life before the foundation of the world, you have nothing to fear. You will be judged by the works of another—by the works of Jesus Christ.

How do you know that your name is in the book of life? Through faith in Christ. Calvin said, "Whosoever then believes is thereby assured that God has worked in him, and faith is, as it were, the duplicate copy that God gives us of the original of our adoption. God has his eternal counsel, and he always reserves to himself the chief and original record of which he gives us a copy by faith."[8] My saving faith is the testimony of God in my life that my name is in the book of the life of the Lamb. Thus, on the final judgment day, all who are in Christ by faith have nothing to fear, because of what Christ has done for them.

8. John Calvin, *Sermons on Ephesians* (Edinburgh: Banner of Truth Trust, 1973), 47.

Now, couldn't someone point to a place like 2 Corinthians 5:10 to argue against what I've just written? Here is what Paul writes: "For we must all appear before the judgment seat of Christ, so that each one may receive what is due for what he has done in the body, whether good or evil." But what does this mean? Is our salvation somehow doubtful? I don't think so, and I think I can show you this by turning back to Matthew 25 again.

Beginning at verse 34 and continuing to verse 40, here is what we read:

> Then the King will say to those on his right, "Come, you who are blessed by my Father, inherit the kingdom prepared for you from the foundation of the world. For I was hungry and you gave me food, I was thirsty and you gave me drink, I was a stranger and you welcomed me, I was naked and you clothed me, I was sick and you visited me, I was in prison and you came to me." Then the righteous will answer him, saying, "Lord, when did we see you hungry and feed you, or thirsty and give you drink? And when did we see you a stranger and welcome you, or naked and clothe you? And when did we see you sick or in prison and visit you?" And the King will answer them, "Truly, I say to you, as you did it to one of the least of these my brothers, you did it to me."

What is fascinating about this scene is that the righteous are surprised. They are surprised that Jesus is commending them. And notice that it is not for what we typically consider the really weighty Christian activities. Jesus does not say, "You translated the Bible into a foreign language. You planted fourteen churches. You raised millions of dollars for charity." Don't get me wrong, these are not bad things at all!

But it's not the big stuff that Jesus commends here—it's the daily love, the daily ministry, that Christ commends. We overlook these kinds of things, but Christ does not. So the only surprise for the righteous in heaven is that Jesus noticed and cared so much about all the little stuff that was involved in just being his servants, doing our best to live for him. And it's going to blow us away how much it means to him.

If you are a Christian, you have works, but you are not justified according to them. You are justified according to the works of the life of the Lamb who was slain. And then, having glorified you, having acknowledged you and admitted you into eternal glory, he will look at you and talk about all the things he did through you.

One thing that this teaches us is that our lives are not about the big achievements. Rather, it is the daily ministry, the love we show, and the things we do for others because we love Jesus. That's what he cares about.

Heaven and the Eternal State

There are a few more questions that people typically have about heaven and the eternal state. Where will heaven be in the end? It will be right here on earth, in the end. The Bible does talk of a place where the disembodied souls are. But after the resurrection and the renewal of the cosmos, the universe will be born again. It's not all new things; it's all things new. The earth will be reclaimed, and the cosmos will be born again. We will dwell there in glorious, resurrected bodies in a garden-temple that will make the original garden pale by comparison.

What will we do in heaven? We will worship. And we will work. Does that surprise you? It shouldn't, for we were made by God to work. We struggle with work because we work under a curse now. But think about this: What do you like to do? What are your hobbies? Don't you enjoy these things? Isn't that why you do them? In heaven, you will enjoy work like that. We will work at cultivating, right beside our heavenly Father.

Lastly, who will be there? John writes these words in Revelation 7:13–14:

> Then one of the elders addressed me, saying, "Who are these, clothed in white robes, and from where have they come?" I said to him, "Sir, you know." And he said to me, "These are the ones coming out of the great tribulation. They have washed their robes and made them white in the blood of the Lamb."

Those who pass through the great tribulation will be in heaven. That is not a reference to a set period of time at the end of the age. John is speaking primarily about the world we're living in. We pass through it, and we wash our robes in the blood of the Lamb.

I want to close with this thought: While it is true that only those whose names are written in the book of life before the foundation of the world will be there, the gospel goes forth today to you. It says that whoever will come, let him come. Take the free gift of the water of life. Believe in the Lord Jesus Christ. It is absolutely imperative now that you should believe in Jesus. Wash your robes. Make them white in the blood of the Lamb.

If you do not, I think the words of Strider in J. R. R. Tolkien's *The Fellowship of the Ring* are appropriate. When he sees the ring wraiths coming for Frodo, he asks the young hobbit, "Are you frightened?" Trembling, Frodo answers, "Yes." Strider looks at him and says, "Not nearly frightened enough."

But if you do turn to Christ, you will have every reason to stop fearing death and start preparing for it, with the hope of eternal life.

9

Evangelical Eschatology, American Style

JEFFREY K. JUE

Seventy weeks are decreed about your people and your holy city, to finish the transgression, to put an end to sin, and to atone for iniquity, to bring in everlasting righteousness, to seal both vision and prophet, and to anoint a most holy place. (Daniel 9:24)

WHEN I TOLD a British friend of mine that I was going to be writing about "Evangelical Eschatology, American Style," he joked, "Yes, you Americans always must have your own style about things." As I hope to show, however, speculation concerning the end times and the desire to understand what the Bible teaches about Christ's second coming are not things that are unique to America. Furthermore, they are not unique to the church of the nineteenth and twentieth centuries.

149

Eschatology in Church History

In the history of the church, there have been many who have wrestled with the prophecies of Scripture from the book of Daniel, as well as the book of Revelation. In particular, some of the famous early church fathers like Justin Martyr, Tertullian, and Irenaeus were well known for their theological contributions, in terms of their understanding of the end times. This was certainly the case as they wrestled with the book of Revelation and, even more specifically, chapter 20, which of course deals with the millennium. In many ways, we could categorize these early church fathers as the first premillennialists in the history of the church.

The interest in prophecy throughout the history of the church has been intense. It began with these early church fathers, but it continued in the medieval period as well. One medieval theologian in particular, Joachim of Fiore, wrestled with these things. He and others were asking what was meant in this mysterious book of Revelation and the various visions contained therein. They wanted to know what those visions meant for the church, in terms of both the present and the future.

The period just prior to the Reformation and on into the Reformation was no different. I think of the famous woodcutting from Albrecht Dürer depicting the four horsemen of the Apocalypse. At the time of the Reformation and in the post-Reformation era, this interest continued unabated, as people were trying to understand what the Lord was doing in the world. This is all very natural, as what many considered to be some of the most traumatic days in the history of Europe were occurring while prophecy was being studied and debated.

In this period, perhaps Luther's interest in prophecy was the most significant. Specifically, he became convinced that there were prophecies being fulfilled in his own lifetime. He was convinced that the so-called Antichrist prophecy had been fulfilled in the person of the Pope. This idea began to shape Protestant apocalyptic thought from that time forward. If one looks at the original version of the Westminster Standards (not the one revised in America), it states that the pope is the Antichrist (WCF, 25.6). So we see the same great interest in apocalyptic or eschatological thinking continuing right into the seventeenth century.

In the modern church, it is not just the theologians who are interested in this, however. We see this fascination ranging all the way from Christian books to *Time* magazine. If you followed the news at all, particularly around the time of what is known as "Y2K," you may remember all kinds of discussions and publications describing this event as the end of the world. As someone in the scholarly world who studies the Apocalypse frequently, I think the height of my popularity was in the year 2000! I received a lot of invitations to speak on this topic, and I thought I should capitalize on the opportunity!

But aside from the Y2K furor, think about the frenzied reading of the popular *Left Behind* series. Those books were always bestsellers on the *New York Times* list, indicating that even the general public, beyond our Christian circles, is very interested in these things. In fact, these books were not just read in America, but translated into numerous languages and read all over the world.

So, simply put, eschatology and end-time speculation have been with us for quite some time. In fact, it is as robust today as it has ever been. Being a seminary professor, I reflect on how this kind of thinking has influenced our theological institutions here in America. Places like Dallas Theological Seminary, Talbot Seminary, and even Trinity Evangelical Divinity School, when they were formed, had a particular eschatology that they wanted to maintain.

But the main question I want to ask is this: is there a belief today that we can say really characterizes or really defines what the evangelical world holds to, in terms of eschatology? I think there is. I will not take the time to explain the options available, since Dr. Venema's chapter in this volume does an excellent job in summarizing them.

American Evangelicalism and Dispensationalism

It can be argued that within the evangelical world, particularly here in America, but not exclusive to it, there is, in fact, an evangelical eschatology. What one finds among evangelical churches, by and large, is that dispensational premillennialism is being taught. Now, if that is the case, how did it become so popular? Also, where did it come from? How did the evangelical world move to that position?

At the outset, let me state that this view of eschatology has never been the majority position in the history of the church. We have seen it come to prominence in the evangelical church only in the last one hundred and fifty years or so. Why did this view became so popular? What was it about this position that caused it to become the majority position in the American evangelical church?

To answer these questions, we have to go back a little bit in history to the eighteenth century. We must examine the ministries of men like John Wesley, George Whitefield, and Jonathan Edwards. These men were instrumental in bringing about the First Great Awakening, both in Britain and in North America. This was a unique time in which revival broke out on these two continents. These individuals in particular defied the established religious norms and left a huge impression on evangelical

Christianity, not just in America, but around the world. Some have gone so far as to say that these men changed the very style of ministry, from their time forward. I think what is meant by this is that the preaching and style of these men changed how others began to preach, both in terms of their method and in terms of their content.

Let us look at how they changed the method first. Wesley and Whitefield were itinerant preachers. They were not men attached to one particular congregation. Jonathan Edwards was a pastor of a local congregation, but Whitefield and Wesley were not. They would travel as itinerant preachers, preaching in many locations. Whitefield, for example, conducted preaching tours up and down the East Coast.

As an aside, since I live in Philadelphia, it is of some interest that one can go to the northeast section of the city and see a placard that marks, to this day, the place where George White-field preached when he visited Philadelphia. The story goes that Benjamin Franklin heard about this great preacher from London who was coming and thought to himself, "I must go hear him speak." Franklin knew that Whitefield always took up a collection at the end of his preaching. Whitefield had a generous heart, especially for orphanages; he was constantly raising money to support these various works. Franklin said to a friend who had joined him, "I'm going to leave my wallet at home, lest I be tempted at the end to put some money in the plate." Franklin said later that he was so moved by Whitefield's preaching that, by the end of the sermon, he was nudging his friend, asking him to lend him some money to put in the plate.

Returning to our study, itinerant preaching is not something we are used to in our day. It consisted of going from place to place and preaching in the open air. This style of preaching was very different than what had come before.

In the second place, let us examine how this changed the content of preaching. If you were to compare Puritan sermons of the seventeenth century with Whitefield's sermons, you would notice quite a difference. A Puritan minister would walk his congregation through whole books of the Bible, expounding (sometimes for very long periods of time!) each and every verse. In contrast to this, the preaching style of Whitefield was vastly different. As an itinerant preacher, he was moving from place to place and essentially preaching what I would like to describe as the "simple gospel." What I mean by this is that men like Whitefield were calling each and every individual in the audience to immediate conversion.

Note the difference, then, between a Puritan minister and someone like George Whitefield. The Puritan moved through various verses, carefully exegeting, again, entire books of the Bible. Of course, he would talk about the gospel, but he would do more than that. He would exegete the various passages and give applications to the congregation. The itinerant preacher, on the other hand, would only be seen by his audience maybe once. And the focus began to be narrowly placed on the simple gospel, with more emphasis on urging the listener to respond immediately. That was the call of ministers like Wesley and Whitefield.

You may know that Wesley and Whitefield eventually parted ways, owing to the fact that Wesley was an Arminian and Whitefield was a Calvinist. Yet, at the same time, their vision for ministry—itinerant preaching, focus on the simple gospel, calling for immediate conversion—remained very much the same. And as a result of this, I would argue, American Christianity moved in a direction that was much more individualist. One individually needed to respond to the gospel. Whitefield and Wesley did not presume that a person was a Christian. They assumed that one needed to hear the gospel and be converted. This kind of preaching pushes the style and influence of that ministry in an individualistic way.

Now let me hasten to add that, on one level, it has always been (and will always be) the case that every Christian must respond to the gospel individually. But in the sixteenth and seventeenth centuries, prior to the Great Awakening, there was much more of an emphasis on the church and being part of a local church. The church was the place where Christians would grow in their understanding of the gospel.

From the time of these men like Whitefield and Wesley onward, Calvinism began to wane. In fact, it practically vanished. What continued on was not Whitefield's Calvinism (truncated though it was), but Wesley's Arminianism, so that what remained was an excessive individualism, linked with an understanding of salvation in which God's sovereignty is downplayed and human decisions are given the supreme place.

What did this do to American Christianity? Well, in the following century, revivalism broke out again, becoming known (appropriately enough) as the Second Great Awakening. This happened particularly as missionaries focused on the expanding West, by which they meant western New York to the Ohio Valley. Probably the most famous preacher of that era was Charles Finney, who wrote a book to serve as a manual for revivalist preachers. He set forth "the new measures" by which to conduct a revival meeting. These new measures included things like setting the proper mood, which meant holding the meeting in a tent in which there would be proper music. Finney complained that the "excitements of the world" were taking people away from God. His solution was to combat the world's excitements with revivalistic excitement.

Finney, of course, was an Arminian, so he believed that people had the ability to choose to believe in Christ. Thus, he introduced things like the anxious bench. This bench was placed at the front of a revival meeting. People would sit or kneel at this bench if they really wanted the revival experience. Finney would preach directly to them, creating excitement that would cause them to respond to the message.

So we could say that the Second Great Awakening added this sensationalist emphasis to the individualistic terms of the First Great Awakening. And it was sensational, in the plainest meaning of that word, during the Second Great Awakening: people were crying, wailing, and falling over in response to the preaching.

The third period of history that sets the stage for us in the nineteenth and twentieth centuries was the rise of modern rationalism, both in America and Europe. The Bible and Christianity were attacked by liberals who reduced Christianity to just one of many religious expressions that ultimately must be verified through strict, rational, historical, and scientific tests. If it doesn't measure up, it cannot be tolerated. Christianity in Europe and America was in the midst of a great theological battle in which German liberal theologians began to apply rationalistic standards to the Bible. They were asking, how can you prove things like the resurrection? Historically, how can one prove things like miracles or the virgin birth? How can you prove that the Bible is inerrant, when in fact it seems to have errors all over it? They claimed we simply couldn't.

The theologians in Germany began to work through the Bible and pull out parts of Christian theology that could not stand up to their scrutiny. In the American church context, this began the phase in which there were great battles, both in the seminaries like Princeton Seminary and in churches like the Presbyterian Church in the U.S.A. The response to this modern rationalism was a division of Christians (very broadly speaking) between what we call the fundamentalists and the modernists. The modernists, as their name implies, wanted very much to go in a liberal direction, while the fundamentalists did not.

George Marsden, who is a historian at the University of Notre Dame, has written very helpfully on this subject. He once asked, "What is a fundamentalist?" He answered: an angry evangelical. What were they angry about? They were angry about liberalism.

Now, in this milieu and associated with the fundamentalists (though, I think, he would have shuddered to be identified with most of them) was J. Gresham Machen, the founder of Westminster Theological Seminary. He wrote a book entitled *Christianity and Liberalism*, in which he argued that liberalism is not Christianity, but a totally different religion. Machen said, basically, that there was no such thing as Christian liberalism. That would be an oxymoron. Liberalism is not Christian at all, according to Machen.

The sad part of this period of American church history is that liberalism swept over the churches like a tidal wave. The result of all this, though, was that it set a course for many evangelicals, particularly in terms of how they understood the Bible. On the one hand, there were German liberal theologians saying, "To understand the Bible, you must study it with all of our modern historical methods that get you underneath or behind the text to the real history. The plain meaning is simply myth." On the other hand, the response by many of the fundamentalists was to adopt a simple literalistic hermeneutic. They said to the liberals, in effect, "Anyone can pick up his or her Bible, read it and understand it, and understand it's true." Not only so, they argued, but as one reads Bible prophecy in this very plain and literal way, one can learn specific details about the future. Following this scheme, one can actually calculate when the prophecies would be fulfilled.

As an aside, it is fascinating to note that during this period of history, in which prophecy was becoming more and more popular as a way of responding to liberals who were denying supernaturalism, the Pentecostal movement was growing as well. Pentecostalism is, generally speaking, theologically conservative. So, they were responding to the liberal denial of supernaturalism by saying, "Look, how can you tell me supernaturalism doesn't exist? Look at the healings! Look at the people speaking in tongues!" Signs and wonders provided another apologetic against those who denied the supernatural character of Christianity.

So the liberalism of the day forced evangelicals into the position of reading the Bible with a literalist hermeneutic. It is not difficult to see, then, how this affects eschatology. Take, for instance, the millennium of Revelation 20. Following the literal reading, this will be a literal, space-time, one-thousand-year period. The same applies to the rest of the book of Revelation: there will be a literal beast, a literal binding of Satan, etc.

Thus, as a result of these various historical contexts—individualism, sensationalism, and the literalistic method—the stage was set for premillennial dispensationalism to grow and become popular in the nineteenth and twentieth centuries. Let me flesh this out a little bit more. In the latter part of the nineteenth century, the writings of John Nelson Darby become extremely popular. Darby was really one of the first men to lay out a dispensational theology, teaching a secret rapture, a future seven-year tribulation period, and a future, literal millennium, among other things. This all comes from a literal reading of Scripture.

From Darby to Today

Now, let us put the pieces together, in terms of Darby's theology. The focus on the individual is now infused with

Darby's doctrine of the rapture. I grew up in a church that was very much taken by this kind of teaching. I can remember the emphasis being on immediate conversion to Christ because the rapture was coming and, of course, you did not want to be left behind to experience that seven-year tribulation period. So this heightens the individualism, as each person seeks to avoid being left behind.

In addition to this was Darby's sensationalism. People became infatuated with the current events of the day, seeing forces moving and events falling into place to prepare for the final events that would precipitate the end. I have seen a website that has a little meter which, depending on the day's current events, gives a percentage estimate of whether or not Christ will be returning soon. It's very sensationalistic. This is also, in part, why even non-Christians read books like the Left Behind series. They are almost "Da Vinci Code–like," with conspiracy theories regarding future events. It is all, again, very sensationalistic.

Perhaps most important was Darby's understanding of the literal interpretation of Scripture. But this can be complicated, as well. This explains the rise of vast and elaborate charts in dispensationalist explanations of the end times. And, though Darby was himself British, his writings gained popularity in America through the work of a number of his followers.

Here in America, this began with men like James H. Brookes. Brookes was born in Tennessee, the son of a minister. He later studied at Miami University of Ohio and even at Princeton Seminary for a while. He became very interested in the writings of Darby and, as a result, began to publish books and pamphlets here in America. In addition to this, he began holding conferences like the Niagara Bible Conference, in which people would gather to be taught Darby's system. Brookes's most famous protégé was Cyrus Ingerson Scofield. C. I. Scofield also grew up in Tennessee and served with distinction in the Confederate Army during the Civil War. After his military service, he studied law and began a political career, serving as a member of the Kansas House of Representatives. He was also, for two years, U.S. District Attorney in Kansas. Thus, Scofield was a very learned and influential man.

Scofield became committed to dispensationalism through Brookes's teaching, eventually becoming a minister of a church in Dallas, Texas. He published a book entitled *Rightly Dividing the Word of Truth*, in which he offered Darby's dispensational teachings in book form. This book was handed out at many of these conferences.

However, Scofield is best remembered for producing the first dispensational reference Bible. The Scofield Reference Bible, interestingly enough, was first published by Oxford University Press. This is noteworthy given that Oxford University Press is not a Christian publishing house. So why would they publish this fundamentalist's Bible? This is where I would argue that market economics enters in—clearly Oxford understood that they would profit from selling the Bible, which they did.

Next we need to take note of Lewis Sperry Chafer. He was a minister in New York and was influenced by Scofield's writings. When Scofield died, Chafer succeeded him at Scofield's church in Dallas. He was instrumental in establishing Dallas Theological Seminary in 1924, which became the flagship school for dispensational theology. Since then, Dallas has graduated generations of pastors trained in this theology.

This brief historical survey explains, albeit only in part, how dispensational theology came to rule the day. But perhaps the most important event energizing dispensational thinking occurred in 1948. On May 14 of that year, British troops withdrew from Palestine and the modern state of Israel was born. Most classic dispensationalists will say that this fulfilled God's promise to give a permanent land to Israel and therefore showed that God had not forgotten his people. This date in 1948 began the fulfillment of that promise, as Israel became a nation again overnight.

But even after 1948, the Cold War also had an impact on the rise of dispensationalism, as communism became the great enemy. It was thought that the Antichrist might arise from one of the communist contries. Communists, of course, were committed to atheism and often persecuted Christians. Many Christians believed that the Antichrist would come from Russia or another communist country. Coupled with this were the great fears of nuclear war and nuclear holocaust, which also fueled the sensationalism which, as we've seen, influenced the dispensationalist system.

In our day, there are many dispensationalists who are convinced that radical Islam is potentially an apocalyptic sign. Some dispensationalists think that Islam is one of the beasts depicted in Revelation, perhaps pointing to the fact that we are again approaching those cataclysmic events described in the book of Revelation.

Implications of Dispensational Eschatology

In the remaining few pages, I will sketch out the implications of this eschatology. To do this, we must first ask if this system has biblical consistency. I will fully disclose where I am coming from: I was raised in a dispensational setting, but have become firmly convinced of the amillennial position. But I want, first and foremost, to evaluate the dispensational system in the light of the whole teaching of Scripture.

As an illustration of dispensational eschatology, I want to focus on Daniel 9. Let me say from the outset that Daniel 9 is the only passage in Scripture that dispensationalists can argue from for a future, seven-year tribulation. It is a good passage to examine when looking at the teaching of dispensationalism, as it will help us see how they handle this passage and what the implications of their view are.

Let me give you a little background for Daniel 9. In 931 BC, upon King Solomon's death, the kingdom of David was divided into Israel in the north and Judah in the south. In 722 BC, the northern kingdom was conquered and the people were carried off into captivity. By 605 BC, the southern kingdom had fallen to Nebuchadnezzar and Judah was sent into exile. Daniel was taken with the exiles of the southern kingdom and eventually served with the high court of Babylon. Babylon fell around 539 BC and so, by Daniel 9, Daniel was under Persian rule.

We find Daniel, in chapter 9, reading from the book of Jeremiah—chapter 25, to be exact. There, Jeremiah prophesies that Israel will be taken into exile for seventy years. Daniel reads that and counts the years, coming to the realization that the prophesied seventy years are about up. So he begins to pray to the Lord, asking him to restore his people, now that the seventy years are almost up. God answers his prayer by sending Gabriel to him, who begins to answer Daniel in verses 24–27. The angel Gabriel gives this response in a somewhat cryptic way. He says that there are seventy weeks about to begin. Now in the literal Hebrew of the original, it doesn't say "weeks"; it simply says "seventy sevens." So, according to Gabriel, the prophecy is being fulfilled according to this format of seventy sevens.

Now, the premillennial dispensationalist looks at that and says, "This is what is going to happen: at the end of this prophecy, when all of the weeks are completed, there will be an end to transgression, an end to sin, and an atonement for iniquity, to bring in everlasting righteousness. Prophecy will be sealed up and the most holy place will be anointed." In other words, dispensationalists believe that this is ultimately going to happen at the end of time. That will be when all of these things are accomplished.

The next question is: what will happen in the meantime? Dispensationalists answer that, in the meantime, we need to work out a time frame from these verses. And here is their explanation: When they see seventy sevens, they say this means seventy times seven. Subsequently, the total time of the prophecy to be fulfilled, if you multiply seventy times seven, is 490 years. Further, the passage goes on to divide those 490 years into three periods. The first period is 49 years (7 x 7); the second period lasts 434 years (62 weeks, or 62 x 7, totaling 434 years). What happens after these two periods? The premillennialist says that this is when the Messiah comes, according to Daniel 9:25.

Given this, if one wants to know when all of this began, count back 483 years from the advent of Christ, which, accepting their time frame, lands one around the time that Cyrus decreed the return of the Jews from exile.

But what about the final seven years? Dispensationalists answer that sometime in the future there will be a seven-year period of tribulation, and when that begins, the counting of years starts up again. Thus, one is left with a huge gap between the fulfillment of the first two periods and the final period. Again, this is the only place in Scripture where they can point to a literal number seven to derive a seven-year tribulation.

But there is another option for understanding this passage. What we need to do in approaching this passage is to understand that there are three themes that intersect for Israel in the Old Testament. These three themes are covenant, promise, and Sabbath. Since Israel is God's covenant people, the covenant contains God's promises, and the sign of the covenant is the Sabbath.

Of course, the Sabbath was instituted even before the fall. From that point forward, it became enshrined in the religious experience of Israel. When the covenant was made with Israel (Ex. 20), they were told to remember the Sabbath day to keep it holy. Exodus 31:13 describes Sabbath keeping as a sign that God is with his people. This passage also says that the sons of Israel were to observe the Sabbath, to celebrate it as a perpetual covenant.

But it was not just one day per week. Their entire calendar was oriented around Sabbaths. In Leviticus 25:1–5, God tells the Israelites to observe land Sabbaths after every sixth year. The Lord would go on to tell Israel in this chapter about seven Sabbaths of years, seven times seven years—periods of forty-nine years. After this, the trumpet was to sound on the tenth day of the seventh month, the Day of Atonement, and a year of liberty would be proclaimed. This was the Year of Jubilee for Israel and the land, a year in which they were to recognize the Lord's blessing. There would be a Day of Atonement and celebration.

Now, when you read the ninth chapter of Daniel, it is tempting to look at it and ask, "Why is the Lord making this prophecy so complicated? If he wanted to say '490 years,' why didn't he simply say '490 years'? Why does God use this cryptic language?" But, now, with this understanding of the background, and especially this kind of language, it makes perfect sense. The Lord has oriented the Israelites' lives around Sabbaths. Thus, when the angel Gabriel gives this prophecy to Daniel, Daniel understands that God is going to take them back to the land, but it will only be a partial restoration. Something even greater is coming.

However, when they do go back to the land, they are to keep the Sabbaths, weekly, yearly, and then the Jubilee year. These Sabbath rests show that God is their God, that he will protect them in the land, and that they will be his people. That is his promise and his covenant.

Returning to the dispensational scheme, the fact that Cyrus was reigning in 539 BC destroys the literal interpretation of this passage, for you cannot argue 483 years ahead to the time of Christ from 539 BC. Instead, I would argue that we need to understand this prophecy symbolically. Gabriel is communicating to Daniel that there is a Sabbath rest coming that will not be like the Jubilee years he experienced in Israel. It will be like ten times that, and the one who will bring in that period of true Sabbath rest is the Messiah himself. There will be completion and fullness to the Messiah's work, which the people had never experienced before. Now Daniel, like some of us, was too shortsighted to see this, but Gabriel was pointing him to the ultimate Sabbath rest found in Christ.

I would further argue that when you look at the details of this chapter, you will see that what separates the final seven is telling us something about Christ, not about some future tribulation. It is telling about Christ, the Messiah, who was cut off in his crucifixion. The destruction of the temple is what ends the Old Testament covenant, which also brings us into the new covenant and the true Sabbath rest, which is not something temporal, but something that will be eternal.

I described this not because I am trying to refute the dispensational position and argue for my position, but simply because I want you to see that a literal reading, which focuses so much on sensational things like the seven-year tribulation, moves the reader away from what is central to every text of Scripture, namely, Jesus Christ. It moves us away from Christ and what he has done for us. As Christians, we are not to live in fear of the tribulation, worrying about whether or not we will participate in the rapture. Instead, we are to focus all of our energy—especially as we read the Bible—on Jesus Christ. We are to focus on what he has accomplished for us and the security that he brings to the people of God.

Think of how this applies to Daniel 9. Remember how Daniel heard about an end to transgressions? That everlasting righteousness would be brought in and atonement made? That the holy place would be anointed and prophecy sealed up (v. 24)? Has Christ not put an end to sin and transgression through his death and resurrection? Has Christ not made atonement for us? Has Christ not given us an everlasting righteousness imputed to us by faith alone? These things are not something awaiting future fulfillment. These things are here with us now in Christ Jesus our Lord.

I want to say, in closing, that although I disagree with the dispensationalist position, my brothers and sisters in that tradition (and I do intentionally call them my brothers and sisters in Christ) bring to the forefront something that is absolutely vital for us to remember. It is the understanding that our Lord is returning. Jesus Christ is coming soon, and we must be prepared for that. I think we can learn something from our dispensationalist brothers and sisters who call us to be ready for that. But, at the same time, being ready should never pull us away from seeing Jesus Christ and his accomplished work as the center of all that we believe and hope for. That must be a part of our eschatology as well. And this is an eschatology that I would hope would not just be an American-style eschatology, but one that would be preached throughout the world until the return of our Savior.

10

The Radical Implications of Eternity

PAUL DAVID TRIPP

For while we are still in this tent, we groan, being burdened—not that we would be unclothed, but that we would be further clothed, so that what is mortal may be swallowed up by life. (2 Corinthians 5:4)

EVERY HUMAN BEING is a theologian. Every human being is a philosopher. Every human being is an archaeologist who will dig through the mound of his existence and seek to make sense of his life. The way that one lives here and now—no matter who that person is—will always be shaped by what he or she believes concerning where we came from and where we are going.

When I was young, our house caught on fire and burned to the ground. I'll never forget the look on my father's face as he gathered me up in his arms, raced through the burning building, and brought me safely to the street. I stood there, shivering in my pajamas, watching our whole world go up in flames. When it was all over, I asked myself, "Is that all there is to life?"

If this is all that life really is—possessions—well, then, let's break out the booze and have a ball! The apostle Paul realized this and presented us with two and only two options. You can see them in 1 Corinthians 15:32: "If the dead are not raised, 'Let us eat and drink, for tomorrow we die.'" That is option one. Option number two is having your life shaped by the words of the old hymn: "But lo! there breaks a yet more glorious day; the saints triumphant rise in bright array; the King of glory passes on his way, Hallelujah!"[1]

Theology for Life

Now, as we think about things like this life and the life to come, let me encourage you to resist the temptation (real as it is) to make theology something you just do with your brain. It must never be something you just do with your intellect. It must never be just outlines and syllogisms and denominational commitments. Theology must be your life. We must reject all forms of theology that are ends in themselves. This is because the gorgeous theology of Scripture that we will be looking at has been revealed by the God of wisdom and glory and grace. It was not meant to be an end in itself, but to be a means to an end. And that end has a radical, awesome claim on every dimension of your life.

Now this means that we must be skilled at understanding the implications of our theology for our everyday experience.

1. "For All the Saints," by William Walsham How (1864, 1875).

We must be good at using the biblical lens to understand the here and now. If you've read Scripture at all, you know that God's people haven't always been good at interpreting life with God's lens!

This leads me to an all-important point: human beings made in the image of God do not live life based on the facts of their experience. We like to think that we do, don't we? However, we live life based on our *interpretation* of the facts. Let me tell you a story to illustrate what I mean.

When my youngest son (who is now grown) was three years old, he knew that his daddy had the title "Doctor" in front of his name. He knew that I saw people for appointments, and he reasoned in his little brain that, because of these facts, I must be a medical doctor. One day he was out in our backyard wandering around like three-year-olds do; after all, they live by the "Columbus method": land and discover! Well, he wandered in front of his older brother, who had a broken rake handle and was hitting stones over the fence into the neighbor's yard. And Ethan took a big swing just as little Darnay walked in front of him, hitting Darnay full swing in the forehead. Of course, Darnay's forehead split open.

I knew something had happened because our daughter, being the family siren, began to scream. It sounded like she was running laps around the yard because the voice repeatedly got distant and then near! I ran to the back door, where I saw Ethan carrying his bleeding brother. Ethan, the perpetrator of the crime, began pleading his case. "Daddy, I am in trouble. How much trouble am I in?" I called for him to put Darnay down on the floor and I yelled for paper towels.

So here's the scene: Nicole, our daughter, is screaming, running laps in the kitchen, while Ethan is plea bargaining: "I will never go in the backyard again; I will never pick up a rake handle again." Now I'm not a squeamish man, but I thought this was a serious injury. So there I was, trying to think of the emergency number 911, and I couldn't form it in my brain. I had all the combinations—111, 999, 919, 191—but I couldn't remember which one it was!

At this point, amidst this chaos, I looked down at little Darnay. To my surprise, he was utterly at peace. His little lips were moving so I put my ear down to his little mouth and I heard him saying over and over again, "I'm just so thankful my daddy is a doctor." Of course, I was thinking, "You are in deep trouble, son; this 'doctor' can't think of a three-digit number at this point!"

Notice that what my youngest son did was intensely human. He was not responding to the facts of his experience; he was responding to his *interpretation* of the facts. The same goes for you and me. You are constantly interpreting.* If you understand this, then you will want to be more self-conscious and intentional in the way that you make sense out of life. You do this by using your theology the way it was meant to be used—as a practical lens to interpret your everyday experiences.

We're going to look at a number of passages in the Bible in this chapter, but I want to start with Numbers 11. It is the account of the children of Israel in the wilderness. They are being sustained by the awesome power of the God who keeps his promises to his children. Look at verses 1–6:

> And the people complained in the hearing of the LORD about their misfortunes, and when the LORD heard it, his anger was kindled, and the fire of the LORD burned among them and consumed some outlying parts of the camp. Then the people cried out to Moses, and Moses prayed to the LORD, and the fire died down. So the name of that place was called Taberah,

because the fire of the LORD burned among them. Now the rabble that was among them had a strong craving. And the people of Israel also wept again and said, "Oh that we had meat to eat! We remember the fish we ate in Egypt that cost nothing, the cucumbers, the melons, the leeks, the onions, and the garlic. But now our strength is dried up, and there is nothing at all but this manna to look at."

This passage teaches us, first of all, that we are, as the children of Israel were, interpreters of our past experiences. The example of God's people here shows what happens when we interpret the past poorly! Indeed, what a horrible interpretation of the past these people had: Egypt, the place of slavery and death, now sounds like a deli. How could they possibly say, "Oh, we had this great buffet at no cost"? At no cost? They had been slaves! They had a distorted view of the past.

But we must take care. Don't be so sure that on Tuesday evening or Wednesday morning, in the mundane things of everyday life, you are interpreting life in a way that's distinctly biblical. What are we talking about here with the Israelites, after all? Not a big issue, actually: it was just the daily menu. But what did they say? Verse 6 tells us: "But now our strength is dried up, and there is nothing at all but this manna to look at." So while they could look to God's faithfulness in the provision of manna, and thus interpret their past correctly (that is, through a biblical lens), they chose instead to grumble and complain. Is that you?

Furthermore, they had a distorted view of the present as well. "How could God do this?" they were asking. "Doesn't God love us? Doesn't God care for us? Why, then, would he give us this boring food to eat, day after day after day?" Now, believe it or not, this passage is a magnificent picture of the covenant love of almighty God. Why would I say that?

Consider this: when Jesus comes, he ties his mission to this episode in the history of God's people. Jesus tells his hearers in John 6:35–38, "I am the bread of life . . . I have come down from heaven." Jesus is telling us that God's provision for his people back then pointed forward to his mission for sinners. God's covenant faithfulness is amazing! But back in the wilderness, the Israelites did not see love or faithfulness in God's provision of manna. They did not see the wise and gracious and almighty hand of God. They had a distorted view of the present. We act like them when we forget that our present circumstances are in the nail-pierced hands of the one whom this event pictures. We, like them, tend to see only trouble in the present.

They also had a distorted view of self. Look at verses 10–15:

> Moses heard the people weeping throughout their clans, everyone at the door of his tent. And the anger of the LORD blazed hotly, and Moses was displeased. Moses said to the LORD, "Why have you dealt ill with your servant? And why have I not found favor in your sight, that you lay the burden of all this people on me? Did I conceive all this people? Did I give them birth, that you should say to me, 'Carry them in your bosom, as a nurse carries a nursing child,' to the land that you swore to give their fathers? Where am I to get meat to give to all this people? For they weep before me and say, 'Give us meat, that we may eat.' I am not able to carry all this people alone; the burden is too heavy for me. If you will treat me like this, kill me at once, if I find favor in your sight, that I may not see my wretchedness."

How's that for a distorted view of self? Is there any evidence that Moses is carrying these people by himself? How about the cloud by day and the fire by night? How about manna appearing every morning as a clear indication of the presence and power and love and faithfulness of God? This man has forgotten his theology. He says, in effect, "What's up with this God?"

So what does this have to do with you? Let me propose this: the reason that, at some moments in your life, you feel alone and overburdened is that you have gospel amnesia. Just like the people here in Numbers, we have a distorted view of self. We forget who we are in Christ.

Next we can see that these people also had a distorted view of God. So do we. We complain about "mundane menus," just like God's ancient people. Here's what the Israelites needed to learn (and us with them): the menu is not mundane, because God's provision is not mundane! Either you are living a life of trust in the sovereign, gracious presence and will of God or you are rejecting his person and his plan and taking your life into your own hands. So something as seemingly insignificant as our daily bread says a lot about our view of God.

How do we know that they were rejecting God? He says as much in verse 20: "You have rejected the LORD who is among you and have wept before him, saying, 'Why did we come out of Egypt?'" So there is no neutrality. What we learn here is this: if you reject God in the mundane moments, you will reject him in the "big moments" of your life. If God doesn't rule your mundane moments, he doesn't rule you at all. We live in the mundane!

Notice what else God says. He says that this is not a little menu issue. He essentially says in verse 20 that they have rejected him in favor of Egypt. So, in the same way, it is possible for us to celebrate eternity on Sunday and reject the entire doctrine on Tuesday evening—in the mundane moments, in other words.

Look at verses 21–23, which are just stunning. God promises meat in response to the people's complaining—and not just a little bit, either:

But Moses said, "The people among whom I am number six hundred thousand on foot, and you have said, 'I will give them meat, that they may eat a whole month!' Shall flocks and herds be slaughtered for them, and be enough for them? Or shall all the fish of the sea be gathered together for them, and be enough for them?" And the LORD said to Moses, "Is the LORD's hand shortened? Now you shall see whether my word will come true for you or not."

What is Moses saying? He is saying, "Lord, don't speak too soon. Have you counted them?" But God has an accurate counting of all the hairs on all the heads of all the people of Israel. And what does God do next? You know the story: he blows in quail (which is not a large bird!) *three feet deep*, for as far as one could travel in a day's journey! How's that for a display of the awesome, providing power of God!

Now, if you functionally—not formally in your theology, but in the mundane affairs of life—have a distorted view of the past, a distorted view of the present, a distorted view of self, and a distorted view of God, then there is no way that whatever you do next will be godly, biblical, or pleasing in God's sight. This is exactly what happened so long ago to Israel. What did they actually ask for? "Take us back to Egypt." That's what they demanded. It is where the wrong interpretation of all these key things leads. They are actually able to look at the whole package from which they have been redeemed as more attractive than being the chosen children of the great covenantally faithful Creator-Redeemer, the Lord of Lords and King of Kings. How shocking!

Typically, we won't think this way in moments when we're thinking about theology in the formal sense. It will happen in the informal moments of everyday life. And here's the point I want to make, related to all of this: your theology of eternity must be something you live out of in the here and now. It is not just something for the future, but something that should inform the way you live in the here and now.

Living the Hope of Eternity

Paul tells us the same thing in 1 Corinthians 15. This is a chapter that deals with living our present lives in light of eternity. In this wonderful passage, Paul says that our hope of eternity (and all the glory that is attached to it) is rooted in the historical fact of the physical resurrection of the Lord Jesus Christ. So it's not that we're conjuring up some dreamy, vague hope. Rather, our belief in eternity, our hope for eternity, is a confident expectation of a guaranteed result. Read that again: it is a confident expectation of a guaranteed result.

That's the first thing. Christianity makes no sense without the historical fact of the resurrection. But Paul argues, in the second place, that Christianity—and all that makes up Christianity—makes no sense without eternity. Verse 19 says: "If in this life only we have hoped in Christ, we are of all people most to be pitied." And then he ends with verse 58, which brackets his entire argument: "Therefore, my beloved brothers, be steadfast, immovable, always abounding in the work of the Lord, knowing that in the Lord your labor is not in vain."

Did you see how that all fits together? Here's Paul's argument: our hope in eternity is sure because it's rooted in the historical resurrection of Jesus Christ. He then reminds us that without Jesus' physical resurrection and its implications for the final resurrection, our faith would be meaningless. But the good news is that Jesus was, in fact, raised from the dead; therefore, "be steadfast, immovable, always abounding in the work of Lord, knowing that in the Lord your labor is not in vain." He is saying, "Don't you understand? This is not something you just sit around and wait for." Paul argues that if you really believe that eternity is a confident expectation of a guaranteed result, then it will radically alter the way you live amongst the harsh realities of life in this fallen world. So you don't just believe in eternity—you *live* it.

Now I would ask you, are you "living" eternity? Husbands, listen to me: Is eternity the reason you're responding the way you're responding to the wife that God has given you? Is it the reason that you are doing radical, gospel-rooted things in your marital relationship—not because you trust your wife, not because life is working for you two, but because you believe in the hopes and promises of eternity? Do you lead an expectant gospel life that causes you to live graciously and perseveringly because you really do believe in the hope of eternity? Do you see how intensely practical a theology of eternity is?

As I have counseled married couples, again and again I have thought to myself that the thing that I needed to do with them was to give them back eternity. Now, I asked some hard questions of husbands. So let me ask wives: Are you living that way with your husband? Are the things that you're doing, the things that you're saying, your love and your patience and your perseverance—are these rooted in the hope that you can get your act together? Are they rooted in the hope that you can establish romance, or in the hope that you can re-create this human being called your husband into somebody who would be more comfortable for you to live with? Or are they rooted in eternity? I wonder if all of us who are married really realize that we could never do anything in the name of the Lord Jesus Christ in our marriages in vain because eternity is guaranteed. If we did realize this, there would be a significant decrease in the writing of marriage-help books!

Now maybe you're thinking, "Paul, I sort of get the concept, but I don't have a clue what it actually means to 'live eternity' in my marriage. I don't know what that means." Well, I want you to do this first thing with me. I want you to turn with me to Revelation 19.

Here's one of the things that I think God is doing in this precious piece of biblical literature: he is inviting us to eavesdrop on eternity. God is inviting us to listen to the voices from the other side. In listening to these voices, God wants to clarify our values for us. This is because there is a war being fought right now for the lordship of your heart. It's a war over what will become valuable to you.

Here is the principle that defines this war: on this side of heaven, it's very hard to keep what is truly important, important in your life. What usually happens is that we do not focus on what really matters. Instead, things that are not nearly as important as they should be rise to levels of utmost importance. They begin to set the agenda for your life in ways that you had never planned. And all of this happens in the most mundane of moments. Let me illustrate.

You are shutting the house down one evening. You go into the kitchen and there on the counter is a plump, still fresh, well-wrapped bagel. In your mind, you immediately name that bagel as your breakfast. You think to yourself, "This is great! I can take a little extra time tomorrow morning. I'll toast that bagel, grab a cup of coffee, and be out of here." A quick, easy breakfast—what could be better? You go to bed that night in the throes of your own bagelism!

You wake up in the morning with your bagelistic intention. As you had planned, you take a little extra time because you know that you have a quick and easy breakfast awaiting you. After taking that extra time, you finally go down to the kitchen.

You walk into the kitchen, look at the counter, and—it's bare. You can feel the emotional temperature changing. You shoot a look at your wife or child that says, "Don't look at me like you don't know what I am puzzled about!" And without moving a step, you bellow, "Who ate my bagel?!"

Now think about this. What is a bagel? It's a hunk of dough with a hole in it. But it's now able to command your emotions. It is able to structure the way you respond to the people that you say you love. This just illustrates the principle that we looked at earlier: on this side of eternity, it's very hard to keep what is truly important, important in our lives.

John Calvin likened the mind of sinful man to "an idol factory." We see the same thought expressed in the Bible, from start to finish. Throughout the New Testament, the writers say to God's people things like "Flee from idolatry" and "Keep yourselves from idols" (1 Cor. 10:14; 1 John 5:21). They were and we are surrounded by all kinds of idolatry.

Again, our idolatry shows up in the mundane moments of life. It might be a discussion with my wife that becomes more than a discussion. I start out sort of wanting unity and love and understanding, but somewhere in the conversation she says something I don't like. Then I quit wanting unity and love and understanding. Instead, I want to win. I want her to say, "You're right! You're the most right person I ever met! I bow beneath your rightness, oh right one!" Or I want the idol of power or the idol of control, or whatever other of the countless idols our mind-factories produce. And God, in his love, allows us to listen to voices on the other side of heaven to right our thinking.

Consider Revelation 19:1–5, which reads,

> After this I heard what seemed to be the loud voice of a great multitude in heaven, crying out,

"Hallelujah!
Salvation and glory and power belong to our God,
   for his judgments are true and just;
for he has judged the great prostitute
   who corrupted the earth with her immorality,
and has avenged on her the blood of his servants."

Once more they cried out,

"Hallelujah!
The smoke from her goes up forever and ever."

And the twenty-four elders and the four living creatures fell down and worshiped God who was seated on the throne, saying, "Amen. Hallelujah!" And from the throne came a voice saying,

"Praise our God,
   all you his servants,
you who fear him,
   small and great."

When the voices from the other side look back on life, and they look back on God's love for them, what do they celebrate? They don't celebrate having the nicest house on the block. They don't say, "We ate the best cuisine; we always had good food to eat." They don't shout, "I had a wife who was beautiful, and she thought I was something special!" or, "I had a great job! I made so much money, and I had so much power!" They are not rejoicing, saying, "I stayed young, way beyond when I should have looked so young." You don't hear any of that stuff. Instead, you hear, "You did it! You did it! You did it! You did it! You are Lord! You are the Savior! Every promise you made, every provision you promised, everything you said you would deliver to your children, you delivered! You are the Almighty, you reign, and we get it." That's what we hear in Revelation 19.

God gives us passages of Scripture like this so that you will live now like you will live then! So I want to ask you a rhetorical question, meant to stimulate your heart: When you look back on a day and say to yourself, "Boy, that was a great day!"—why do you say that? Is it because it was truly a great day in light of eternity? Be honest. Was it a great day because it was another step in the awesome plan of God, who is moving his world? Was it a day when something I said or something I did pleased him?

Eternity versus the Idols

You simply cannot squeeze the values of Revelation 19 into the temporary, pleasure-rooted, materialistic values of Western culture. It doesn't work. But most evangelical Christians have bought into this value system. It is not just "the world out there"—it is us, Christians.

Think about it. We stand in front of huge closets full of clothes and say, "I don't have a thing to wear!" We are eating way more than we need to eat and paying the price for it. We have acquired paralyzing debt.

This all comes from the interpretation of life that says, "If this is all there is, then let's keep dancing." That's not a problem for "out there"; it's a problem for the people of God. And it is time—I say this in pastoral love—that we *stopped it*. What do we have to offer the world if we are bowing down to their idols with them?

I want you to know that this is my struggle too. I was in northern India on a four-day research tour of Hinduism. I was going to do extensive ministry in India, and I needed to understand the culture. I was in Rishikesh, which is at the base of the Himalayas. It is where the Ganges flows out of the Himalayas. Rishikesh is one of the high holy cities of Hinduism; and as the Ganges comes out of the Himalayas, it glows like the Caribbean Sea. It is amazing. One can understand how these animistic people would think that the Ganges must be a holy river.

I was in a temple that was purported to be one of the purest incarnations of Shiva. It was the most shockingly ugly religious scene I have ever witnessed. This may embarrass some people, but I need to be a bit graphic here. The idol that confronted me in that temple was a twenty-foot high representation of a male sexual organ. I saw dirt-poor Indian pilgrims come into that temple and immediately begin to weep. They would throw themselves down on the floor, grab the base of the idol, and kiss it. So many people had performed this ritual that the base was dented from the kisses.

As I witnessed this, I talked (through an interpreter) with an Indian family, which had practically no earthly goods. Over the last several months, this family had literally walked *four hundred miles* to get to that temple. And they were deeply moved in the presence of that horrible thing!

I found myself running out of there, trying to escape the darkness. I was running down a dirt path, praying these words: "God, I thank you that I am not like these people." And then it hit me: I am *just like* these people! The idolatry of our comfortable, materialistic Western culture, although "nonreligious," is as nauseous to our Lord as that image was to me that day. When this thought hit me, I began to weep. I could only pray, "Lord, help me. Lord, help me. Lord, help me. Lord, help me. Lord, help me."

Incidents like this deeply persuade me that the values of eternity are meant to be a principal defense against the idols that seek to entrap us on our way to eternity. So run to passages like Revelation 19 again and again to get your values corrected and clarified. Your heart is under attack. It's not just that you desire the wrong thing—it's inordinate desire for even a good thing. That's right: even a desire for a good thing becomes a bad thing when that desire becomes a ruling principle. My heart must only be ruled by King Christ.

Living for Eternity

So the question becomes: what values are you living? Be honest. What set of values shapes your decisions? What set of values shapes the way you think about what you would like a week to be like or your life to be like? What values shape the way you think about relationships? What values shape the way you think about yourself? What values shape the way you use your leisure time? What values shape the way you use your money and your possessions? Are you living for eternity?

Let's listen to the apostle Paul again. In 2 Corinthians 5:1–6, he says:

> For we know that if the tent, which is our earthly home, is destroyed, we have a building from God, a house not made with hands, eternal in the heavens. For in this tent we groan, longing to put on our heavenly dwelling, if indeed by putting it on we may not be found naked. For while we are still in this tent, we groan, being burdened—not that we would be unclothed, but that we would be further clothed, so that what is mortal may be swallowed up by life. He who has prepared

us for this very thing is God, who has given us the Spirit as a guarantee. So we are always of good courage.

What does the apostle say should be the two responses of my heart as I am living in light of eternity? Here is the first one: groaning. But it's not the groaning of complaint. I think we're too good at that. We groan all the time because things don't work the way we want. Our food doesn't taste the way we want it to, our clothes don't look the way we want them to, and people don't respond the way we want them to. Our children don't turn out the way we want them. My wife doesn't always respond the way that I want her to respond. We are experts at the groaning of complaint.

This kind of groaning is evil and self-centered. It focuses on the here and now. It says that life is all about my pleasure. It proclaims, "I'm in the center of my world, and life right now must work for me because life right now is all there is." It's an absolute rejection of the gospel, and we are guilty of thinking like this.

But the groaning Paul is speaking about here is a groaning of longing. It is a longing to be with Christ, to be done with sin, to be less attached to this world and its ensnaring idols. This is the very opposite of evil and self-centered groaning. And, again, I am not immune to the evil groaning.

My wife, Luella, and I spend Monday together; I travel almost every weekend, and so Monday is our day together. One Monday, Luella had to be away for what she was doing, and we had agreed that this was important. We were going to meet up at four o'clock. In my self-centered little world, the time we agreed upon was precise and unbending. For Luella, it was a rough estimate. At 4:05, I began to get upset. At 4:07, I called her. "Where are you?" Not, "Hello, dear, how has your day been?

I've been praying for you. I love you so much. Where are you?"
No, just a very annoyed "Where are you?" She said, "Well, I'm
stuck in traffic." Now, I didn't say, "Well, that's a shame. I feel
bad that you're in traffic." Again, one sentence: "How long are
you going to be?" At this point, because she is deeply insightful,
she said, "Are you upset?" Caught, I replied, in a nonchalant
kind of way, "No, I am not upset. I am not upset at all. I'm just
wondering when you're going to get here, because this is our
day." Of course I was upset! I was upset because I want life to be
comfortable and everything to work my way, on my schedule.
And when it doesn't, I complain and get upset and mistreat
people I love.

If you are honest, you do not want me to play a recording
of your groaning last month. You probably weren't groaning
with longing. You and I do not, in and of ourselves, long for
anything beyond a pampered existence in the here and now. So
we groan, to be sure. But we groan because the here and now is
not working according to our sovereign will. And that is not at
all what Paul is talking about.

The second quality that the apostle is talking about is courage. He reasons that if we believe in the absolute guarantee of
eternity, then we will live with courage. We will not do so simply because circumstances are favorable, or because the people
around us are affirming us, but because God is our Father. His
plan has been set in motion, and it will not be thwarted. So
we seek to do good and live with courage. We do this, not
because good things are always affirmed or recognized or easy,
but because we live under the wise counsel of a sovereign, saving God. That's Christianity. It means I'm good to you on your
bad days. I don't say, "Do you know what it's like to live with
you? I've got enough problems without you spilling your stuff
on me." Instead, I react with gospel love because the good that

I'm doing is motivated by eternity—not by the satisfactions of the present moment.

I like the general atmosphere of this passage in 2 Corinthians because talking about tents is pilgrim talk. Paul, with his language of groaning and longing and courage and tents, is speaking of a pilgrim lifestyle. If you're a pilgrim who is constantly moving, what keeps one foot going in front of the next? Longing. After all, a good pilgrim is not going to stop halfway. A good pilgrim, because he longs for his destination, keeps going forward. He may groan in the hardship. But he or she keeps going. This is the perfect illustration of our lives as Christians.

Pilgrims have courage, because nothing is going to keep them from reaching their destination. Like them, we get robbed, it rains, and we get lost. But we keep going forward because we have a vision of what is to come. But the problem for most of us here in the West is that we don't know what it's like to be pilgrims because we live in comfort and ease. Most of us have never had pilgrim experiences. I think the closest that we can get to this pilgrim analogy in modern Western culture is camping, the main purpose of which is to make you long for home.

When you begin the camping trip, you're excited. You love the fact that you are actually sleeping in a portable dwelling called a tent. It's pretty cool. By day three, that tent has odors you can't identify. They go from bad human to subhuman. When you cook that first meal, you say, "Doesn't food cooked over an open flame taste different?" But by the third day, when you have collected all the wood that is close, you begin to look for a sign that gives you permission to cut down the nearest tree. You're tired of gathering all that wood.

You start to notice that your back is hurting you from lying on that hard surface and you're thinking, "I wonder if the other people who are with me are thinking what I'm thinking: maybe we could go home early." You begin to dream of your refrigerator, which has food in it that isn't spoiled. You recall your stove that requires no firewood. You think about your soft mattress. You are suddenly longing for home. Camping has done exactly what it's supposed to do for you!

But maybe even this analogy isn't good in our culture anymore. Now we don't even camp in tents. We camp in $150,000 Winnebagos, with a kitchen and a 42-inch flat screen. Your camping experience can be better than home! No wonder we don't long for anything. So, in our lives, we've said, "I'm going to make life as comfortable and as pleasurable as possible. I'm going to meet all of my desires and wants." We have no concept of being pilgrims.

If you are a pilgrim, it's a paired down, lean existence. Having a pilgrim mindset is how to "live eternity." Perhaps our houses are too big. Perhaps we've weighed ourselves down with too many clothes, too much food, and too much entertainment. We have forgotten who we are. We have ceased being pilgrims.

The Grace of Refinement

I want to look at one more passage as we think about how to "live eternity," 1 Peter 1:3–9:

Blessed be the God and Father of our Lord Jesus Christ! According to his great mercy, he has caused us to be born again to a living hope through the resurrection of Jesus Christ from the dead, to an inheritance that is imperishable, undefiled, and unfading, kept in heaven for you, who by God's power are being guarded through faith for a salvation ready to be revealed in the last time. In this you rejoice, though now for a little while, as was necessary, you have been grieved by various trials, so that the tested genuineness of your faith—more precious than gold that perishes though it is tested by fire—may be found to result in praise and glory and honor at the revelation of Jesus Christ. Though you have not seen him, you love him. Though you do not now see him, you believe in him and rejoice with joy that is inexpressible and filled with glory, obtaining the outcome of your faith, the salvation of your souls.

Notice what Peter is saying in verses 3–5. He is saying that there is the grace of the new birth and the guarantee of future hope. Peter's interest is in the here and now, and that's why verse 6 says, "In this you rejoice, though now . . ." Here's what Peter wants us to ask ourselves: is how we live in the here and now shaped by the truth that we have a guarantee of eternity?

But we ask, "What is it that God is doing in the meantime? If that's my hope, then why doesn't God just deliver it to me right away? Why don't I come to Christ and disappear? Wouldn't that be easier? What's the meaning of the here and now? If eternity is our hope, why wait?" These are good questions. In fact, one of our main questions as Christians seems to be, "What is it that God is doing in the here and now? What is the here and now all about in light of eternity?"

Well, when Peter thinks of how to describe the here and now, with all the vocabulary of human language that he has available to him, he chooses these three words: *grieved*, *trial*, and *test*. *Grieved*, *trial*, and *test* are three words that we generally do not want to characterize our lives!

I'm sure no one prays (at least not regularly!), "Lord, my life has been way too easy. If you can send some grief, trials, and tests, I would be so happy and feel so loved." So why does Peter choose these three words to describe God's purpose for us in light of eternity? Well, Peter uses a wonderful example for us. It's an example from metallurgy. When a miner mines a metal, he digs up ore. Ore is not very attractive, nor is it very usable, because it has imperfections in it. Those imperfections rob the ore of its strength and beauty. So the metallurgist knows that he must add white hot heat and a catalytic agent, boiling those imperfections out of the metal. He does this until it reaches its highest state of strength and beauty.

Now, when you come to Christ, you are an "ore-rific" Christian. I didn't say "horrific"—I said "ore-rific"! You have imperfections in you that rob you of your strength and beauty. God couldn't possibly remain a loving, faithful Redeemer, committed to his eternal purpose to make you holy and blameless in his sight, yet leave you in your state of "ore-dom."

So, Peter is giving us a rich illustration of how to understand the here and now in light of eternity. He is basically saying that God, in the grandeur and glory of his redemptive love, will boil you. I like to put it this way: God will take you where you never intended to go, in order to produce in you what you could not achieve on your own. He will drive you beyond your strength. He will drive you beyond your wisdom. He will drive you beyond your own imagined righteousness, because he knows that true righteousness only begins when you come to the end of yourself. We must not think of trials and griefs and testings as a sign of God's unfaithfulness and inattention. They are a sure sign of his eternal commitment and covenantal love.

There are many times when we go through those kinds of things and we cry out, "Where is the grace of God?" All the time, however, we are in fact receiving the grace of God. But it's not the grace of relief, nor is it the grace of release. Relief will come someday, and release will come someday, but what you actually need now is the grace of *refinement*. We must, in light of eternity, begin to teach and comfort and encourage one another with the "theology of uncomfortable grace." Very often, this side of eternity, God's grace comes to you in uncomfortable forms—because that's exactly what you need.

So Peter is saying, "You must not think of now as a destination; now is not the destination." You cannot live with a destination mentality. The destination mentality says, "This is all we have—let's get as much as we can get. Let's get as much pleasure, as much affirmation, as much power, and as much money as we possibly can."

There is a wonderful Sri Lankan theologian, Vinoth Ramachandra, who wrote *Gods That Fail*.[2] And one of the things that Ramachandra says is that the most dangerous idols of all are those that are easily Christianized. That's what has happened to us here in the West: we have "Christianized" our gods of money, pleasure, and security. And this, as Ramachandra says, makes them all the more dangerous.

Preparing for a Christ-centered Eternity

We must remember that this life is not a destination. It is a preparation for the final destination, so that our faith, though tested, will result in praise, glory, and honor at the revelation of Jesus Christ. Here's what eternity tells us, and it is deeply humbling: eternity is not about me. It is about Christ. The greatest, deepest mystery and joy in my life is and ever will be that I have been included in Christ. This broken, lost, sinful,

2. Vinoth Ramachandra, *Gods That Fail* (Downers Grove, IL: InterVarsity Press, 1997).

rebellious man will actually be a trophy that will point to the glory of the grace of King Christ. That's what the here and now is about.

What is the agenda of preparation? It is not personal, temporal happiness, but grace initiated, which results in God-glorifying holiness. That's what now is about. Every time you envy the luxury of another person, you're an eternity amnesiac. Every time you argue somebody into a corner with uncomfortable personal power and argumentation, you're an eternity amnesiac. Every time you spend more than you ever should spend, you're an eternity amnesiac. Every time you're angry because somebody somehow is in your way, you're an eternity amnesiac. Every time you step across God's holy law to do what you want to do, say in gossip or looking at pornography, you're an eternity amnesiac. Every time you crave the position of another person, you're an eternity amnesiac. Every time you eat till your belly hurts, you're an eternity amnesiac. Peter tells us that these kinds of behavior don't make sense in light of eternity.

So now is pilgrim time. It is preparation time. It is wartime. It is "being formed into the image of the Lord Jesus Christ" time because eternity is a guaranteed home. There is a guaranteed destination. Victory is sure. Put one foot in front of the other, even if you feel like you're just plodding along. Do so with deep longing and courage because Jesus *is* and he is King.

God help us never to make eternity just be an item in our theology. May he instead make it formative of every desire, every thought, every word, and every action. May we not live like we're waiting in a dentist's office, waiting for God to finally call us in. Instead, let us live in courage, hope, and longing, with every word and every deed formed by a confident expectation of a guaranteed result.

So where do you live eternity? You live it in the family rooms, kitchens, hallways, bedrooms, boardrooms, and events of everyday life. Like I said at the beginning, you will either live "This is all there is, so let's dance" or you will live "But lo! there breaks a yet more glorious day." Press forward with longing and courage because the future is guaranteed.

ALLIANCE®
OF CONFESSING EVANGELICALS

What is the Alliance?

The Alliance of Confessing Evangelicals is a coalition of Christian leaders from various denominations (Baptist, Presbyterian, Reformed, Congregational, Anglican, and Lutheran) committed to promoting a modern reformation of North America's Church in doctrine, worship, and life, according to Scripture. We seek to call the twenty-first-century Church to a modern reformation through broadcasting, events, publishing, and distribution of Reformed resources.

The work centers on broadcasting: *The Bible Study Hour* with James Boice, *Every Last Word* featuring Philip Ryken, *God's Living Word* with Bible teacher Richard Phillips, and *Dr. Barnhouse & the Bible* with Donald Barnhouse. These broadcasts air daily and weekly throughout North America as well as online and via satellite.

Our events include the Philadelphia Conference on Reformed Theology, the oldest continuing national Reformed conference in North America, and many regional events, including theology and exposition conferences and pastors' events, such as reformation societies that continue to join the hearts and minds of church leaders in pursuit of reformation in the Church.

reformation21 is our online magazine—a free "go-to" theological resource. We also publish *God's Word Today* online daily devotional, MatthewHenry.org, a source on biblical prayer, Alliance books from a list of diverse authors, and more.

The Alliance further seeks to encourage reformation in the Church by offering a wide variety of CD and MP3 resources featuring Alliance broadcast speakers and many other nationally recognized pastors and theologians.